Feminisms and Educational Research

Philosophy, Theory, and Educational Research Series

Editor: Nicholas C. Burbules, University of Illinois at Urbana-Champaign

This series is designed to explore the dominant philosophical and theoretical positions influencing educational research today. A distinguished international group of scholars explains these positions in straightforward terms, making these books suitable for courses in educational research methods and foundations in educational research. The series editor is active as a coauthor with each book to ensure their overall consistency in tone and format, and to encourage the discussion of issues that cut across books so that they can be read comparatively as well as independently. Each volume shows how a particular philosophical and theoretical position affects the methods and aims of educational research and provides specific examples of research that show these orientations at work. The emphasis is on lively, accessible, but theoretically sound explorations of the issues. These books are of interest not only to educational researchers but to anyone in education wanting to understand what these various "isms" are about.

TITLES:

Feminisms and Educational Research
by Wendy Kohli and Nicholas C. Burbules

Poststructuralism and Educational Research
by Michael A. Peters and Nicholas C. Burbules

Pragmatism and Educational Research
by Gert J. J. Biesta and Nicholas C. Burbules

Postpositivism and Educational Research
by D. C. Phillips and Nicholas C. Burbules

Feminisms and Educational Research

Wendy R. Kohli
and
Nicholas C. Burbules

ROWMAN & LITTLEFIELD EDUCATION
Lanham • New York • Toronto • Plymouth, UK

Published by Rowman & Littlefield Education
A wholly owned subsidiary of The Rowman & Littlefield Publishing Group, Inc.
4501 Forbes Boulevard, Suite 200, Lanham, Maryland 20706
www.rowman.com

10 Thornbury Road, Plymouth PL6 7PP, United Kingdom

British Library Cataloguing in Publication Information Available

Library of Congress Cataloging-in-Publication Data

The hardback edition of this book was previously cataloged by the Library of
Congress:

Kohli, Wendy.
    Feminisms and educational research / Wendy Kohli and Nicholas C. Burbules.
        p. cm.
    Includes index.
    1. Feminism and education—Research.   2. Feminist theory.   I. Burbules,
Nicholas C.   II. Title.
    LC197.K65 2012
    370.72'082—dc23

                                                            2011035355

ISBN: 978-1-4758-0526-0

Contents

Series Preface

THIS BOOK WITH WENDY KOHLI IS THE FOURTH IN ROWMAN & LITTLEFIELD'S series Philosophy, Theory, and Educational Research. Contemporary educational research has seen an explosion of new methodologies and approaches to inquiry. Many of these approaches have drawn from philosophical or theoretical positions that underlie their choices of research methods, aims, and criteria of validity. Yet, the substance of these philosophical or theoretical assumptions is not always made clear to readers, and so it is difficult for them to judge those assumptions for themselves.

This series is designed to explore some of the dominant philosophical and theoretical positions influencing educational research today, in a manner that does justice to the substance of these views and shows their relevance for research purposes and practices. Each volume will show how a particular set of philosophical and theoretical positions affects the methods and aims of educational research; and each will discuss specific examples of research that shows these orientations at work. The emphasis is on lively, accessible, but theoretically sound explorations of the issues. These books are intended to be of interest not only to educational researchers but to anyone in education wanting to understand what these various "isms" are about.

This series features a distinguished international group of scholars. It is important for the reader to know that the first author of each volume has had primary responsibility for conceptualizing and drafting the text. The series editor has played a very active role in selecting the topics and organization for each volume, has interacted regularly with the first author as the text has been drafted, and has had a relatively free hand in revising the

vii

text and adding or suggesting new material. This is more than the role that editors normally play, and so second authorship seemed the appropriate appellation. But the predominant voice and point of view for each volume in the series is the first author's. It could not be otherwise, since no coauthor could advocate equally all the positions, many of them mutually inconsistent, argued for in these volumes.

—Nick Burbules
June 23, 2011

Acknowledgments

I WOULD LIKE TO ACKNOWLEDGE THE MATERIAL SUPPORT OF FAIRFIELD University and the intellectual and emotional support from my feminist colleagues near and far.

Most importantly, I am indebted to my husband, Philip Bennett, who has remained steadfast in his commitment to me and my work, providing the humor and nurturing to see this project to its long-awaited completion.

—Wendy Kohli

CHAPTER 1

Introduction

WE WRITE THIS BOOK AT A TIME WHEN RESEARCH IN THE SOCIAL AND human sciences in general, and educational research in particular, is suffering from the aftereffects of "methodological fundamentalism"—a conservative ideological commitment institutionalized through federal policies and practices (Denzin & Lincoln, 2005, p. xi). This period began with the resurgence of a so-called "'gold standard' for producing knowledge . . . based on quantitative, experimental design studies" (p. xi) that incited dialogue, debate, and distress in scholarly educational circles. In particular, those engaged in a range of qualitative and postpositivist studies were enraged at the narrowing of the definition of scientifically based research that was promoted by the National Research Council and enforced in legislation like the No Child Left Behind Act (Feuer, Towne, & Shavelson, 2002, p. 4).

Against the background of this "worldwide audit culture with its governmental demands for evidence-based practice and the consequent (re) privileging of scientistic methods" (Lather, 2007, p. 2), we see this volume, along with other books in this series, as among the many attempts to resist the backlash of "narrow scientificity" (p. 2) and to reassert the value and necessity of multiple, alternative modes of inquiry that better fit the plurality and complexity of our human social world. Feminist inquiry, critical race theory, poststructuralist thought, and other "counterhegemonic, decolonizing" research paradigms offer multiple avenues to critical understanding, transformation, and action (Denzin & Lincoln, 2005, p. x).

1

The overall aim of this book is to introduce the philosophical and theoretical ideas that constitute the various strands of feminism and to articulate the implications of these strands for our understanding of the conduct of educational research.[1] In analyzing the relation between feminism(s) and educational research,[2] we will attend to the work of more recent feminists—from the field of education, as well as philosophy, sociology, and literary theory—and focus on the epistemological, ontological, and political questions that surround gendered knowledge production and inquiry. In the past thirty years, the field of education has produced some of the most cutting-edge theorizing in feminist research generally and has fostered innovative feminist research methods and methodologies.[3] Perhaps this is due, in part, to the predominantly feminized nature of the teaching profession and the prominence of feminist scholars in many schools of education. In our last chapter, we discuss some of those who have made significant differences in feminist and educational theory and research.

WHAT IS FEMINISM?

It may not be self-evident what we mean by *feminism*, a term appropriated in many different ways and to different purposes. Hence, chapter 2 explains the range of understandings and positions feminists have taken over time. New volumes abound indicating not only the diversity of perspectives within feminist scholarship but also how the field has reconceptualized its categories.[4] Gone are the days when it was possible (or acceptable) to make simple distinctions by labeling a variety of feminism as "liberal," "socialist," or "radical," a common practice in the 1960s and 1970s. As Sandra Lee Bartky (1990, p. 11), among other feminist theorists, noted, "Contemporary feminism has many faces . . . divided along ideological lines" that include liberal, socialist-Marxist, and radical feminism. But such classifications have had to be expanded and transformed to incorporate cultural feminism, lesbian feminism, psychoanalytic feminism, feminism of difference, ecofeminism, poststructural feminism, postcolonial feminism, and critical race feminisms, among others. By naming the many forms of feminism, we do not want to commit the sin of making a "rather tired and liberal gesture, which declares plurality at the level of naming" (Ahmed et al., 2000, as cited in Lather, 2007, p. 173). Instead, we hope to "argue the case for differences that cannot be reconciled into this pluralism" (p. 173). The problem is not so simple as adding an "s" at the end and referring to a variety of "feminism(s)," but to acknowledge the multiple and conflicting internal conversations that have always typified feminist theory and practice—and to see it as partly constitutive of feminism as a theory and practice to foster and accommodate such conversations.

A historical overview of these shifting tides within feminism must include not only the so-called first and second waves but also the newer third wave of theorizing by a young generation of feminists who are countering the antifeminist backlash of right-wing "postfeminists."[5] Second-wave feminism, and the challenges to it by postmodern, postcolonial, and poststructuralist thought, receives the most focused attention here, since these debates have shaped, and continue to shape, current discourse about gendered experience, identity, and subjectivity—and these have proven some of the areas most fertile for investigation in the context of education.

In the early days of second-wave feminism, there was a political commitment to end women's oppression and to challenge male domination (or patriarchy) in institutions and personal relations. Women concentrated on eliminating gender discrimination in the workplace by working on policy issues such as the Equal Rights Amendment, attaining wage equity, and providing decent, affordable child care. Much of the feminist research to support those goals during this period occurred within the social sciences, particularly in applied sociology. More recently, a shift has taken place in feminist theorizing and politics. There has been a movement away from what some feminists see as "monocausal and totalizing theories of patriarchy" (Kemp & Squires, 1997, p. 6). With the influence of postmodernism, postcolonialism, and poststructuralism, feminist theory has turned to language, power, and culture to explore the complexity and contingency of gender (at the same time, feminist work has partly shaped and informed work within postmodern, postcolonial, and poststructuralist theory).

What has come to be known as the crisis of representation has provided a "profound rupture" in how research is done (Denzin & Lincoln, 2005, p. 18). This "turn to language," with its focus on symbolization and representation, affected the kind of political questions asked by feminist theorists. Kemp and Squires (1997, p. 6) suggest that "the focus of such questioning is not primarily the central question of early second wave feminism—'what is to be done?'—but rather the more reflexive, 'what is the basis of my claim to knowledge?' and 'who is the "I" that makes such a claim?'" Nevertheless, we will stress here, feminist theorizing and research have nearly always had a close connection with issues of transformed politics, practices, and personal relations.

PHILOSOPHICAL CONCERNS AND COMMITMENTS

In chapter 3, we address the epistemological and ontological shifts and debates that have occurred in feminism over the past two decades, and address current topics at the forefront of feminist theorizing. For example, Patti Lather (2007, p. 8) in her book, *Getting Lost: Feminist Efforts Toward a Double(d) Science*, resists the tendency of the "successor sciences" promoted by some feminists seeking a better science than mainstream science. Working with and against "post" discourses, Lather indicates that "the central investment of [her] book is in coming to terms with the complexities involved in the 'post' turn in the human sciences" (p. 5). In order to address this question of whether feminist inquiry results in "better" or "truer" accounts, we must traverse the terrain of feminist epistemology, which still has relevance for questions of (feminist) educational research.

Feminist epistemology came on the scene with full force in the 1980s and 1990s as feminism challenged the traditional conceptions of knowledge and knowing that pervade mainstream (male) philosophy. This is not to say that there has been a monolithic view of epistemology throughout the history of philosophy; most certainly there have been diverse positions on the relation of the knower to the known and the possibility of "objectively" knowing the world, including work done in phenomenology, hermeneutics, and critical theory, which has long problematized any simple, correspondence view of truth and representation (Denzin & Lincoln, 2005, p. 12). But in this volume, we focus particularly on the feminist challenges to traditional research and epistemology.

Early feminist critiques focused specifically on the dominance of "male" experience and the systematic exclusions of women as both subjects and objects of knowledge. Key components of this feminist criticism included unpacking the connections between knowledge and power, and the valuing of subjective personal experience as an undeniable aspect of knowledge and knowing. All of this was done in the context of confronting the categories of rationality, objectivity, certainty, and universality handed down to us by the Cartesian legacy in Western philosophy. But this early critique did not yet entail the formulation of an alternative "feminist" epistemology.

Later, feminist standpoint theory emerged as an important element of a feminist epistemology. With no small amount of indebtedness to Marxist historical materialism, feminists argued that women, as members of a subordinated group, have the potential for a more complete view of the "truth" because their perspective is more capable of recognizing the dynamics of society as they are, not from the interested perspective of those with a stake in legitimating and preserving those dynamics.[6] However, this version of standpoint theory was subjected to reevaluation and critique from several quarters, including black and lesbian feminists speaking from their own "silenced standpoints," who objected to the assumed unity or privileging of women's experience per se.[7]

Once multiple standpoints were recognized, the entire project of standpoint theory had to be rethought: there can be "no a priori epistemological grounds for deciding a hierarchy of standpoints—of the superordinate right or correct one over and against subordinate standpoints" (Stanley, 1997, p. 277). Furthermore, it became ever clearer that the feminist solidarity politics of the early second wave were no longer as persuasive: class, race, ethnicity, and sexuality provided for a more complicated, disrupted view of women and women's experience. *Difference* came to the table and with it came discussions about the social construction of differences, versus essentialized views. The ontological question of "what and who is a woman?" (Kemp & Squires, 1997, p. 10), prompted by psychoanalysis and poststructuralist theory, and "the view of subjectivity as discursively constructed and multiple" (Nicholson, 1997, p. 5), set the stage for energetic debate across a range of ideological feminist positions.

FEMINIST RESEARCH

Following this historicized mapping of feminism and feminist theory, we proceed to a discussion of the feminist research process. Chapter 4 focuses on such questions as: What is the role of a feminist researcher? What kinds of questions does this researcher ask? What ethical, social, or political commitments accompany this type of research? Given the plurality of feminisms and the many feminist challenges to traditional scientific and social scientific inquiry, there must be, necessarily, a plurality of approaches to feminist research: approaches dependent on the assumptions brought to the endeavor by the researcher.

In the 1970s, "'feminist research' was defined as a focus *on* women, in research carried out *by* women who were feminist, *for* other women" (Stanley & Wise, 1990, p. 21). Furthermore, there was an essentializing of research methods: quantitative methods were identified as "male" and qualitative methods as "feminist" (Stanley & Wise, 1990, p. 21; Oakley,

2000, p. 33). Finally, it was assumed that feminist researchers were engaged in their work for explicitly political purposes—they wanted to change the life situations of women (Stanley & Wise, 1990, p. 21).

In retrospect, it is more apparent that the research coming out of the early second wave of feminist history was undertheorized: it "relied on over-generalized and under-researched categories such as 'woman,' 'gender,' 'structure'" (Stanley & Wise, 1990, p. 21). Both *feminism* and *research* were used in monolithic, totalizing ways. With the advent of postmodern and poststructuralist theorizing, and the disruption of unitary concepts, feminist research was challenged to reflect the complex and contradictory characteristics of the social world as lived. Significantly, the main focus of feminist research shifted from "women's experience" to "gender" itself. For many feminists, "very simply, to do feminist research is to put the social construction of gender at the center of one's inquiry" (Lather, 1991, p. 71).

The social construction of gender has influenced many of the key issues in recent feminist theorizing and research. For example, it appears in one of the recurring sites of contestation in mainstream research literature: the "paradigm wars" between quantitative and qualitative methods (Oakley, 2000, p. 23). The controversy takes a particular form within feminist research, where some scholars continue to dispute whether the quantitative-qualitative dichotomy reflects an underlying gender bias. Some feminist scholars "claim that quantitative research techniques . . . distort women's experience and result in a silencing of women's own voices" (Jayaratne & Stewart, 1991, p. 85). The counterargument suggests a worry over the subjective bias of the researcher (p. 85). But still others think the nature of this debate is problematic because of its polarizing and essentializing tendencies (p. 94), and its similarly dichotomous and essentializing characterization of how gender operates.

This qualitative-quantitative debate points in turn to one of the persistent themes in the philosophy of the social sciences: the problem of objectivity. As noted earlier, many feminist scholars have challenged the legacy of Cartesianism that assumes a split between the objective world of the known and the subjective world of the knower. They insist that this discourse of objectivity is profoundly masculinist and serves to mask and promote male domination. Yet there are other feminists who argue that feminism would be ill served if traditional views of rationality and objectivity were abandoned. For example, some feminist empiricists argue that "traditional research methods can be used to our advantage" to change public opinion and to create the social change for women that feminists want (Jayaratne & Stewart, 1991, p. 100). More recently, Patti Lather (2007, p. 71) has argued for the need to go beyond the often-rehearsed dichotomies to a "postscientistic sort of objectivity." We explore how traditional issues of objectivity in research, the nature of evidence, and the criteria for warranted assumptions are understood within different feminist research paradigms.

By recollecting the feminist epistemological frameworks that have been discussed in previous chapters, chapter 4 provides an overview of the methodological debates within feminist research and their potential impact on feminist educational research. In so doing, this chapter unpacks some assumptions about methods and methodology, relying on Sandra Harding's (1987b, p.1) useful distinctions. Yet we also look at advances in the "postpost" work of Lather (2007) and others. In the course of this exploration of feminist inquiry, we examine the (sometimes controversial) connections between science, politics, and action, as well as the relation between the researcher and the researched (Mies, 1991, p. 61).

These broad themes are followed by an overview of particular research methodologies that feminists have adopted, including (critical) ethnographies, oral life histories, autobiographies, biographies, and collaborative research, as well as other more experimental "performances" of research (Olesen, 2005, p. 253). Attention is given to the philosophical assumptions underlying these different methods, particularly in light of postmodern claims about the partiality, relationality, and undecidability of knowledge.

FEMINIST EDUCATIONAL RESEARCH

Feminists, particularly second wave Anglo-American feminists in the United States, England, Canada, Australia, and New Zealand, have long seen education as a critical site for emancipatory feminist research (Acker, 1994; Olesen, 2005; Weiner, 1995). A good deal of this second-wave feminist research in education fell under the early rubrics of liberal, socialist, and radical feminism. Those who engaged in liberal feminist scholarship were generally interested in "equal opportunities . . . socialization and sex-stereotyping; . . . [and] sex discrimination" (Acker, 1994, p. 45). Socialist-Marxist feminist educational researchers began to challenge the liberal framework, incorporating analyses of production, reproduction, and sexuality into their critiques (Weiner, 1995, p. 57). Radical feminist educators focused their inquiries on two major problems: "(1) the male monopolization of culture and knowledge; and (2) the sexual politics of everyday life in schools" (Acker, 1994, p. 50). They believed, as stated by Mary O'Brien, that "the goal of a feminist education . . . is not equality in knowledge, power and wealth, but the abolition of gender as an oppressive cultural reality" (cited in Acker, p. 50).[8]

Of course, as noted earlier, this tripartite categorization of feminist scholarship has been disrupted by postmodern, postcolonial, and poststructuralist theories. There is now, for example, a great deal of exciting educational research employing a feminist-Foucauldian frame that examines, among other things, the discursive production of femininity, masculinity, and power (Britzman, 1997; Ellsworth, 1997; Jones, 1996; Mayo, 2000; Middleton, 1998; Miller, 1992; Munro, 1998; Pillow, 2004; Ropers-Huilman, 1998; St. Pierre, 2000). We will be drawing on the work of several feminist poststructuralists, as well as some postcolonial scholars, to elucidate this transformation of feminist scholarship. While chapter 5 reviews some of the early research on women, schooling, and gender (Acker, 1994; Arnot, 1981, 2002; Arnot & Weiner, 1987; Biklen, 1995; Biklen & Pollard, 1993; Weiner, 1995; Weiner & Arnot, 1987), more attention is given to those feminist works that develop a multifaceted understanding of gendered subjectivities discursively produced in educational settings. In doing so, we hope to attend to the value of such postempirical research for educators who may have come up against the limits of more modernist scholarship.[9]

This final chapter recounts several distinctive forms of feminist educational research in order to give the reader a grasp of why particular scholars—even those who might not be feminist themselves—find this an important and fruitful line of investigation. The educational feminist work highlighted here is theoretically sophisticated and trend setting. We explore a few examples in detail, including the groundbreaking work of Leslie Roman (1992, 1993), who developed a feminist materialist approach to ethnographic research; the innovative research of Wanda Pillow (2000, 2004) who employs Foucauldian-influenced feminist genealogy in her research on educational policy and practice; the black feminist research/praxis of Annette Henry (1993, 1998); the research on "endarkened feminist epistemology" created by Cynthia Dillard (2000, 2006); and the queer theory/research of Deborah Britzman (1995, 1997), deCastell and Bryson (1997), and Cris Mayo (2004, 2007, 2008). As noted, we believe that such work exemplifies theoretical, methodological, and analytical innovations and insights that ought to be of interest to educational researchers of all types.

NOTES

1. From the start, we want to acknowledge the limitations of relying too heavily on Western feminist perspectives. As Olesen (2005), McCann and Kim (2003), Mohanty (2004), Smith (2000), Mohanty, Russo, and Torres (1991), Anzaldua (1990), Anzaldua and Moraga (1983), and others remind us, to have a vital, effective women's movement, women of color from around the world, North and South, must inform the intellectual and political work of feminist scholars in this age of transnational globalization.

2. We acknowledge the objection of Patti Lather who, like her citation of Sara Ahmed et al. (2000), prefers "feminism in the singular" (Lather, 2007, p. 172n).

3. See, for example, the work of Patti Lather, Deborah Britzman, Leslie Roman, Leslie Bloom, Michelle Fine, Valerie Walkerdine, Kathleen Weiler, Gabby Weiner, Sandra Acker, and a host of others.

4. We think here of such texts as *Feminisms: A Reader*, edited by Maggie Humm (1992); *Feminisms in the Academy*, edited by Domna Stanton and Abigail Stewart (1995); *Feminist Thought: A More Comprehensive Introduction*, Rosemarie Tong (1998); *The Second Wave: A Reader in Feminist Theory*, edited by Linda Nicholson (1997); *Feminisms*, edited by Sandra Kemp and Judith Squires (1997); *The Routledge Companion to Feminism and Postfeminism*, edited by Sarah Gamble (2004); and *Feminist Theory Reader: Local and Global Perspectives*, edited by Carole McCann and Seung-Kyung Kim (2003).

5. The date generally given to the first wave spans 1830–1920. The second wave begins in 1960 and continues to the present. The third wave has emerged on the scene in such volumes as *Third Wave Agenda*, edited by Leslie Heywood and Jennifer Drake (1997) and *Third Wave Feminism: A Critical Exploration*, edited by S. Gillis, G. Howie, and R. Munford (2004). Ann Brooks's 1997 analysis, *Postfeminisms: Feminism, Cultural Theory and Cultural Forms*, answers the more conservative "antifeminism" that emerged in the 1990s.

6. See, for example, Hartsock's (2004) classic, "The Feminist Standpoint: Developing the Ground for a Specifically Feminist Historical Materialism," Harding's (1987a) *Feminism and Methodology*, Harding's (2004) most recent edited volume, *The Feminist Standpoint Theory Reader: Intellectual and Political Controversies*, and Jaggar's (1983) *Feminist Politics and Human Nature*.

7. See, for example, Patricia Hill Collins (2000) in *Black Feminist Thought: Knowledge, Consciousness and the Politics of Empowerment* and Monique Wittig (1981), "One Is Not Born a Woman."

8. See, for example, Kathleen Weiler's (1988) *Women Teaching for Change: Gender, Class and Power* for a thorough overview of feminist analyses of gender and schooling.

9. See, for example, Bloom (1998); Bloom and Munro (1995); Britzman (1995, 1997, 2000, 2003); Bryson and deCastell (1993); Davies (1989); deCastell and Bryson (1997); Jones (1989, 1993, 1996, 2003); Lather and Smithies (1997); McWilliam (1994); Miller (2005); Munro (1998); Walkerdine (1990).

REFERENCES

Acker, S. (1994). *Gendered education: Sociological reflections on women, teaching and feminism.* Buckingham, UK: Open University Press.

Ahmed, S., Kilby, J., Lury, C., McNeil, M., & Skeggs, B. (Eds.). (2000). *Transformations: Thinking through feminism.* London: Routledge.

Anzaldua, G. (Ed.). (1990). *Making face, making soul: Creative and critical perspectives by feminists of color.* San Francisco: Lute Books.

Anzaldua, G., & Moraga, C. (Eds.). (1983). *This bridge called my back: Writings by radical women of color.* New York: Kitchen Table, Women of Color Press.

Arnot, M. (1981). Culture and political economy: Dual perspectives in the sociology of women's education. *Education Analysis,* 3(1), 97–116.

Arnot, M. (2002). *Reproducing Gender? Essays on educational theory and feminist politics.* London: Routledge/Falmer.

Arnot, M., & Weiner, G. (Eds.). (1987). *Gender and the politics of schooling.* London: Hutchinson.

Bartky, S.L. (1990). *Femininity and domination: Studies in phenomenology and oppression.* New York: Routledge.

Biklen, S.K. (1995). *SchoolWork: Gender and the cultural construction of teaching.* New York: Teachers College Press.

Biklen, S.K., & Pollard, D. (1993). *Gender and education: Yearbook of the National Society for the Study of Education* (92nd ed.). Chicago: University of Chicago Press.

Bloom, L. (1998). *Under the sign of hope: Feminist methodology and narrative interpretation.* Albany: State University of New York Press.

Bloom, L., & Munro, P. (1995). Conflicts of selves: Nonunitary subjectivity in women administrators' life history narratives. In J. Hatch & R. Wisniewski (Eds.), *Life history and narrative* (pp. 99–112). London: Falmer Press.

Britzman, D. (1995). Is there a queer pedagogy? Or, stop reading straight. *Educational Theory,* 45(2), 151–165.

Britzman, D. (1997). What is this thing called love? New discourses for understanding gay and lesbian youth. In S. DeCastell & M. Bryson (Eds.), *Radical interventions: Identity, politics and difference/s in educational praxis* (pp. 184–207). Albany: State University of New York Press.

Britzman, D. (2000). "The question of belief": Writing poststructural ethnography. In E. St. Pierre & W. Pillow (Eds.), *Working the ruins: Feminist poststructural theory and methods in education* (pp. 27–40).

Britzman, D. (2003). *Practice makes practice: A critical study of learning to teach.* Albany: State University of New York Press.

Brooks, A. (1997). *Postfeminisms: Feminism, cultural theory and cultural forms.* London: Routledge.

Bryson, M., & deCastell, S. (1993). Queer pedagogy: Praxis makes im/perfect. *Canadian Journal of Education,* 18(3), 285–305.

Casey, K. (1993). *I answer with my life: Life histories of women teachers working for social change.* New York: Routledge.

Collins, P.H. (2000). *Black feminist thought: Knowledge, consciousness, and the politics of empowerment.* New York: Routledge.

Davies, B. (1989). *Frogs and snails and feminist tales: Preschool children and gender.* Sydney: Allen and Unwin.

deCastell, S., & Bryson, M. (Eds.). (1997). *Radical interventions: Identity, politics and difference/s in educational praxis.* Albany: State University of New York Press.

Denzin, N., & Lincoln, Y. (Eds.). (2000). *The Sage handbook of qualitative research* (2nd ed.). Thousand Oaks, CA: Sage.

Denzin, N., & Lincoln, Y. (Eds.). (2005). *The Sage handbook of qualitative research* (3rd ed.). Thousand Oaks, CA: Sage.

Dillard, C. (2000). The substance of things hoped for, the evidence of things not seen: Examining an endarkened feminist epistemology in educational research and leadership. *International Journal of Qualitative Studies in Education,* 13(6), 661–681.

Dillard, C. (2006). When the music changes, so should the dance: Cultural and spiritual considerations in paradigm proliferation. *International Journal of Qualitative Studies in Education,* 19(1), 59–76.

Ellsworth, E. (1997). *Teaching positions: Difference, pedagogy and the power of address.* New York: Teachers College Press.

Feuer, M., Towne, L., & Shavelson, R. (2002). Scientific culture and educational research. *Educational Researcher,* 31(8), 4–14.

Fine, M. (1992). *Disruptive voices: The possibilities of feminist research.* Ann Arbor: University of Michigan Press.

Fonow, M., & Cook, J. (Eds.). (1991). *Beyond methodology: Feminist scholarship as lived research.* Bloomington: Indiana University Press.

Gamble, S. (Ed.). (2004). *The Routledge companion to feminism and postfeminism.* London: Routledge.

Gillis, S., Howie, G., & Munford, R. (Eds.). (2004). *Third wave feminism: A critical exploration.* Hampshire, UK: Palgrave Macmillan.

Harding, S. (Ed.). (1987a). *Feminism and methodology: Social science issues.* Bloomington: Indiana University Press.

Harding, S. (1987b). Introduction: Is there a feminist method? In S. Harding (Ed.), *Feminism and methodology: Social science issues* (pp. 1–14). Bloomington: Indiana University Press.

Harding, S. (Ed.). (2004). *The feminist standpoint theory reader: Intellectual and political controversies.* New York: Routledge.

Hartsock, N. (2004). The feminist standpoint: Developing the ground for a specifically feminist historical materialism. In S. Harding (Ed.), *The feminist standpoint theory reader: Intellectual and political controversies* (pp. 35–53). New York: Routledge.

Henry, A. (1993). Missing: Black self-representation in Canadian educational research. *Canadian Journal of Education,* 18(3), 206–222.

Henry, A. (1998). *Taking back control: African Canadian women teachers' lives and practices.* Albany: State University of New York Press.

Heywood, L., & Drake, J. (Eds.). (1997). *Third wave agenda: Being feminist, doing feminism.* Minneapolis: University of Minnesota Press.

Humm, M. (Ed.). (1992). *Feminisms: A reader.* Hertfordshire, UK: Harvester Wheatsheaf. (Also published in 1992 as *Modern feminisms: Political, literary, cultural.* New York: Columbia University Press.)

Jaggar, A. (1983). *Feminist politics and human nature.* Totowa, NJ: Rowman and Allanheld.

Jaggar, A. (Ed.). (1994). *Living with contradictions: Controversies in feminist social ethics.* Boulder, CO: Westview Press.

Jayaratne, T. E., & Stewart, A. (1991). Quantitative and qualitative methods in the social sciences: Current feminist issues and practical strategies. In M. Fonow & J. Cook (Eds.), *Beyond methodology: Feminist scholarship as lived research* (pp. 85–106). Bloomington: Indiana University Press.

Jipson, J., Munro, P., Victor, S., Froude Jones, K., & Freed-Rowland, G. (1995). *Repositioning feminism and education: Perspectives on educating for social change.* Westport, CT: Bergin and Garvey.

Jones, A. (1989). The cultural production of classroom practice. *British Journal of Sociology of Education,* 10(1), 19–31.

Jones, A. (1993). Becoming a "girl": Post-structuralist suggestions for educational research. *Gender and Education,* 5, 157–167.

Jones, A. (1996). Desire, sexual harassment, and pedagogy in the university classroom. *Theory into Practice,* 35(2), 102–109.

Jones, A. (2003). The monster in the room: Safety, pleasure and early childhood education. *Contemporary Issues in Early Childhood,* 4(3), 235–250.

Kemp, S., & Squires, J. (Eds.). (1997). *Feminisms.* Oxford, UK: Oxford University Press.

Ladson-Billings, G. (1995). Toward a theory of culturally relevant pedagogy. *American Educational Research Journal,* 32(3), 465–491.

Ladson-Billings, G. (2000). Racialized discourses and ethnic epistemologies. In N. Denzin & Y. Lincoln (Eds.), *Handbook of qualitative research* (2nd ed., pp. 257–278). Thousand Oaks, CA: Sage.

Lather, P. (1991). *Getting smart: Feminist research and pedagogy with/in the postmodern.* New York: Routledge.

Lather, P. (2007). *Getting lost: Feminist efforts toward a double(d) science.* Albany: State University of New York Press.

Lather, P., & Smithies, C. (1997). *Troubling the angels: Women living with AIDS.* Boulder, CO: Westview.

LeCompte, M., Millroy, W., & Preissle, J. (Eds). (1992). *The handbook of qualitative research in education.* San Diego: Academic Press.

Mayo, C. (2000). The uses of Foucault. *Educational Theory, 50*(1), 103–116.

Mayo, C. (2004). Queering school communities: Ethical curiosity and gay-straight alliances. *Journal of Gay and Lesbian Issues in Education, 1*(3), 23–36.

Mayo, C. (2007). Queering foundations: Queer and lesbian, gay, bisexual and transgender educational research. *Review of Research in Education, 31,* 78–94.

Mayo, C. (2008). Obscene associations: Gay-straight alliances, the Equal Access Act, and abstinence only policy. *Sexuality Research and Social Policy, 5*(2), 45–55.

McCann, C., & Kim, S. (Eds.). (2003). *Feminist theory reader: Local and global perspectives.* London: Routledge.

McRobbie, A. (1991). *Feminism and youth culture: From Jackie to Just Seventeen.* Boston: Unwin Hyman.

McWilliam, E. (1994). *In broken images: Feminist tales for a different teacher education.* New York: Teachers College Press.

Middleton, S. (1998). *Disciplining sexuality: Foucault, life histories and education.* New York: Teachers College Press.

Mies, M. (1991). Women's research or feminist research? The debate surrounding feminist science and methodology. In M. Fonow & J. Cook (Eds.), *Beyond methodology: Feminist scholarship as lived research* (pp. 60–84). Bloomington: Indiana University Press.

Miller, J. (1992). Exploring power and authority issues in a collaborative research project. *Theory into Practice, 31*(2), 165–172.

Miller, J. (1993). Constructions of curriculum and gender. In S. Biklen & D. Pollard (Eds.), *Gender and education* (p. 43). Chicago: University of Chicago Press.

Miller, J. (2005). *Sounds of silence/breaking: Women, autobiography, curriculum.* New York: Peter Lang.

Mohanty, C.T. (2004). *Feminism without borders: Decolonizing theory, practicing solidarity.* Durham, NC: Duke University Press.

Mohanty, C.T., Russo, A., & Torres, L. (Eds.). (1991). *Third world women and the politics of feminism.* Bloomington: Indiana University Press.

Munro, P. (1995). Multiple "I's": Dilemmas of life-history research. In J. Jipson, P. Munro, S. Victor, K. Froude Jones, & G. Freed-Rowland (Eds.), *Repositioning feminism and education: Perspectives on educating for social change* (pp. 139–152). Westport, CT: Bergin and Garvey.

Munro, P. (1998). *Subject to Fiction: Women teachers' life history narratives and the cultural politics of resistance.* Buckingham, UK: Open University Press.

Nicholson, L. (Ed.). (1997). *The second wave: A reader in feminist theory.* New York: Routledge.

Oakley, A. (2000). *Experiments in knowing: Gender and method in the social sciences.* Cambridge, UK: Polity Press.

O'Brien, M. (1983). Feminism and education: A critical review essay. *Resources for Feminist Research,* 12(3), 291–300.

Olesen, V. (2000). Feminisms and qualitative research at and into the millennium. In N. Denzin & Y. Lincoln (Eds.), *The Sage handbook of qualitative research* (2nd ed., pp. 215–255). Thousand Oaks, CA: Sage.

Olesen, V. (2005). Early millennial feminist qualitative research: Challenges and contours. In N. Denzin & Y. Lincoln (Eds.), *The Sage handbook of qualitative research* (3rd ed., pp. 235–278). Thousand Oaks, CA: Sage.

Pillow, W. (1997). Exposed methodology: The body as a deconstructive practice. *International Journal of Qualitative Studies in Education,* 10(3), 349–363.

Pillow, W. (2000). Deciphering attempts to decipher postmodern educational research. *Educational Researcher,* 29(5), 21–24.

Pillow, W. (2002). Gender matters: Feminist research in educational evaluation. *New Directions for Evaluation,* 96, 9–26.

Pillow, W. (2003a). "Bodies are dangerous": Using feminist genealogy as policy studies methodology. *Journal of Educational Policy,* 18(2), 145–159.

Pillow, W. (2003b). Confession, catharsis, or cure? Rethinking the uses of reflexivity as methodological power in qualitative research. *International Journal of Qualitative Studies in Education,* 16(2), 175–196.

Pillow, W. (2004). *Unfit subjects: Educational policy and the teen mother.* New York: Routledge/Falmer.

Roman, L. (1988). Intimacy, labor and class: Ideologies of feminine sexuality in the punk slam dance. In L. Roman, L. Christian-Smith, & E. Ellsworth (Eds.), *Becoming feminine: The politics of popular culture* (pp. 143–184). London: Falmer.

Roman, L. (1992). The political significance of other ways of narrating ethnography: A feminist materialist approach. In M. LeCompte, W. Millroy, & J. Preissle (Eds.), *The handbook of qualitative research in education* (pp. 555–594). San Diego: Academic Press.

Roman, L. (1993). Double exposure: The politics of feminist materialist ethnography. *Educational Theory,* 43(3), 279–308.

Roman, L., Christian-Smith, L., & Ellsworth, E. (Eds.). (1988). *Becoming feminine: The politics of popular culture.* London: Falmer.

Ropers-Huilman, B. (1998). *Feminist teaching in theory and practice: Situating power and knowledge in post-structural classrooms.* New York: Teachers College Press.

Smith, B. (Ed.). (2000). *Global feminisms since 1945: Re-writing histories.* London: Routledge.

Stanley, L. (Ed.). (1990). *Feminist praxis: Research, theory and epistemology in feminist sociology.* London: Routledge.

Stanley, L. (1997). Recovering women in history from feminist deconstructionism. In S. Kemp & J. Squires (Eds.), *Feminisms* (pp. 274–277). Oxford, UK: Oxford University Press.

Stanley, L., & Wise, S. (1990). Method, methodology and epistemology in feminist research. In L. Stanley (Ed.), *Feminist praxis: Research, theory and epistemology in sociology* (pp. 20–60). London: Routledge.

Stanton, D.C., & Stewart, A. (Eds.). (1995). *Feminisms in the academy.* Ann Arbor: University of Michigan Press.

St. Pierre, E. (2000). The call for intelligibility in postmodern educational research. *Educational Researcher*, 29(5), 25–28.

St. Pierre, E., & Pillow, W. (2000a). Introduction: Inquiry among the ruins. In E. St. Pierre & W. Pillow (Eds.), *Working the ruins: Feminist poststructural theory and methods in education* (pp. 1–24). New York: Routledge.

St. Pierre, E., & Pillow, W. (Eds.). (2000b). *Working the ruins: Feminist poststructural theory and methods in education.* New York: Routledge.

Tong, R. (1998). *Feminist thought: A more comprehensive introduction.* Boulder, CO: Westview.

Walkerdine, V. (1990). *School girl fictions.* London: Verso.

Weiler, K. (1988). *Women teaching for change: Gender, class and power.* South Hadley, MA: Bergin and Garvey.

Weiner, G. (1995). *Feminisms in education: An introduction.* Buckingham, UK: Open University Press.

Weiner, G., & Arnot, M. (Eds.). (1987). *Gender under scrutiny:* London: Hutchinson.

Wittig, M. (1981). One is not born a woman. *Feminist Issues*, No. 2, 47–54. Reprinted in C. McCann & S. Kim (Eds.). (2003). *Feminist theory reader: Local and global perspectives* (pp. 249–254). London: Routledge.

CHAPTER 2

What Is Feminism?

DEFINITIONAL PROBLEMS

It is easy to ask but difficult to answer the question, "What is feminism?" given the plurality of contested views that exist currently in feminist theory and research. As noted in chapter 1, scholarship reveals not only a diversity of perspectives but also a fundamental reconceptualization of the field (Olesen, 2005; Lather, 2007). To complicate matters further, some feminists have resisted—on feminist principles—rigid definitions and categories. Lorraine Code (2000), editor of the *Encyclopedia of Feminist Theories*, describes the difficulty well:

> Producing [this encyclopedia] is a challenging project, for the scope and diversity of feminism(s) are wide, their manifestations disparate, complex and changing. Yet the very idea of an encyclopedia assumes a possibility of order and a degree of constancy: of clear, neatly delineated representations of discrete subject matters. Thus to select and fix a terminology that could adequately represent so vitally evolving a set of theories and theorists smacks of that same old authoritarian imposition of mastery and control that feminists of the second wave have worked to resist. (p. xv)

So in trying to answer the lead question of this chapter, not only must we contend with multiple feminist viewpoints, but we also risk violating feminist principles. This is a particularly difficult conundrum for one of us, who is a self-identified feminist author, and the other, who is an ally to feminist issues. If it violates feminist principles to impose categories on others' beliefs and theories, how can we make the claim that we are all "feminists" engaging in "feminist" scholarship and practice? Who are "we"?

Why?

The answer was no easier for Juliet Mitchell and Ann Oakley (1986) when they compiled a volume to elucidate the problem. For them, posing the question, "What is feminism?" marked "an investigation into something we assume we know" (p. 1). They pointed to the "quicksand that lies beneath simplistic attempts to say what feminism is—and is not" (p. 3). In a similar vein, Mary Evans (1997, p. 9), writing about the situation in the 1990s, insists "that the term 'feminism' . . . needs more careful consideration than it received in the heady days of the late 1960s and early 1970s." She goes on to say that "the very word now demands a measure of deconstruction" to address the diversity of the movement's constituencies (p. 9).

Oakley, Mitchell, Code, and Evans are not alone in grasping the difficulty of defining feminism in all its plurality and diversity. Rosalind Delmar (1986) concurs when she argues that "the fragmentation of contemporary feminism bears ample witness to the impossibility of constructing modern feminism as a simple unity" (p. 9). The feminist historian Barbara Caine (1997) reminds us that "the current emphasis in feminist theory and women's studies on the need to recognize diversity and difference amongst women, and to accept the existence of many different and even conflicting emancipatory projects and feminisms in place of any unitary 'feminism,' alerts one to the inevitable prescriptiveness involved in any attempt at definition" (p. 2). The Australian scholar Chris Beasley (1999) declares that feminism is "a troublesome term" (p. ix) that requires more "than any fixed definition that you may find in a dictionary or encyclopedia" (p. xii). She argues persuasively that the process of defining feminism(s) is as important as coming to any final "clear-cut definition" (p. xiv).

bell hooks, however, appears more skeptical and less sanguine when she laments this situation in her oft-cited essay, "Feminism: A Movement to End Sexist Oppression":

A central problem within feminist discourse has been our inability to either arrive at a consensus of opinion about what feminism is or accept definition(s) that could serve as points of unification. Without agreed upon definition(s), we lack a sound foundation on which to construct theory or engage in overall meaningful praxis. (hooks, 1984, p. 17; 2003, p. 50)

Although we are sympathetic to hooks's desire for a unified voice, we also want, like Beasley (1999, p. xiv), "to provide the sense of a field alive with possibilities." That is not to deny the importance—if not necessity—of naming at least some of the conceptual boundaries of feminism. So, in an arguably feminist approach, we will locate or situate feminism within a conversation of many voices in an effort to grasp the complexity and fluidity, and yet also the provisional commonality, of the field. This includes the theorizing done by a "third-wave" generation of young women who "have been shaped by struggles between various feminisms as well as by cultural backlash against feminism and activism" (Heywood & Drake, 1997, p. 2). In this sense, the contestation over, and resistance toward settling, the very question before us seems to be constitutive of feminism as much as any particular definition one might proffer: feminism is a conversation, and sometimes a debate, over what it means to be a woman, to be a feminist, in the face of acknowledged differences and diversities. Here again the development of theory is guided by reflections about how theoretical stances play out in terms of actual social relations and practices (communicative and otherwise). The political task of establishing feminist solidarity implicates, and is implicated by, theoretical choices.

One way of approaching this issue, though provisionally, is through a descriptive, historical lens. By recounting some of the major shifts and repositionings within feminism,[1] perhaps we will observe some "family resemblances" (à la Wittgenstein) that will lead to a more philosophically rich understanding of feminist theory and research, if not a unitary definition. And maybe we will demonstrate what Christina Hughes (2002, p. 3) refers to as a "conceptual literacy": Hughes acknowledges the profound influence of postmodern and poststructural theory, particularly in relation to "the significance of language in understanding the changing nature of meaning" (pp. 2–3). Highlighting the difficulty of "fixing meanings," Hughes argues for a conceptually literate researcher who is sensitized "to the political implications of contestation over the diversity of conceptual meanings" (p. 3).

As noted, we are trying to be sensitive not only to the epistemological and methodological implications arising from the multiple understandings of feminism, but also to the political ones. After all, it has been argued that feminism has at its very core a political agenda. For example, Kemp and Squires (1997, p. 4) insist that "the single most distinguishing feature of feminist scholarly work has been its overtly political nature." It is this explicitly political dimension of feminism that raises controversial issues for traditional researchers: defining things (and who gets to define them) is itself a political problematic.

So, for example, returning to Mitchell and Oakley (1986), we find in their search for a definition of feminism that they wanted to continue the task started by other feminists "to discover and create a history both for women and their intellectual and practical struggle" (p. 1). They were doing this as part of a critique of the "biology is destiny" assumption that informed the "radical feminism" of the 1960s and 1970s. In particular, Mitchell and Oakley (1986, p. 1) argued with de Beauvoir's classic text, *The Second Sex,* which suggested that as a biological category, *woman* "suffers from a singular oppression which knows of no historical period that precedes it." What follows from the critique by Mitchell and Oakley is the assertion that as long as "woman cannot be fixed as an identity beyond the biological female, neither can feminism have a unified definition" (pp. 2–3). Consequently, to understand women—and presumably feminism—one needs to situate them in particular historical contexts. This historicity affords a more complete, if more complicated, picture of both the history of women and the boundaries of feminism.

In accepting the need to historicize the concept of "woman," we ask, as did the authors in the Mitchell and Oakley (1986) collection, "whether it makes sense to assume *any necessary* unity within feminism" (p. 3, emphasis added). Rosalind Delmar (1986), for one, acknowledges this same problem when she says, "It has become an obstacle to understanding feminism, in its diversity and in its differences, and in its specificity as well" (p. 8). She admits, "It is certainly possible to construct a base-line definition of feminism" (p. 8). However, "*at a theoretical level, agreements are uncovered only by the exploration of differences*" (p. 10, emphasis added). And Caine (1997) argues, "the question of feminism itself—of what it means and what it encompasses—has become immensely more complex and almost impossible to answer with any degree of certainty" (p. 2). More recently, Estelle Freedman (2002) echoes this sentiment when she asks, "Given its changing historical meanings, is there any coherence to *feminism* as a term? Can we define it in a way that will embrace its variety of adherents and ideas?" (p. 7).

Yet, at the same time, these and many other feminists—for a variety of reasons—have in fact "assumed that there was a potentially unificatory point of view on women's issues" (Delmar, 1986, p. 10). Delmar offers this provisional definition of a feminist:

> someone who holds that women suffer discrimination because of their sex, that they have specific needs which remain negated and unsatisfied, and that the satisfaction of these needs would require a radical change (some would say a revolution even) in the social, economic and political order. (p. 8)

Olive Banks (1981), in a very inclusive definition, suggests that feminists are "any groups that have tried to *change* the position of women, or the ideas about women" (p. 3). Banks suggests that this broad approach can express "the different faces of feminism [in a way that] has seemed more fruitful than adopting a narrow definition" (p. 3).

The Concise Glossary of Feminist Theory gives a minimal definition from which to work: "the term implies the identification of women as systematically oppressed; the belief that gender relations are neither inscribed in natural differences between the sexes, nor immutable, and a political commitment to their transformation" (Andermahr, Lovell, & Wolkowitz, 1997, p. 76). Allison Jaggar (1994), in a volume on the controversies within feminism, provides yet another working definition. She "identifies feminism with the various social movements dedicated to ending the subordination of women . . . people, male or female, count as feminist if and only if they are sincerely committed to this goal" (p. 2). Jaggar justifies this approach because she believes "it makes political sense to employ a definition that is as uncontroversial and widely acceptable as possible" (p. 2). Jaggar is committed to avoiding sectarianism and to "creating a safe space for in-house discussion among feminists" (p. 2).

Similarly, Estelle Freedman (2002) devised a comprehensive "four-part definition":

> Feminism is a belief that women and men are inherently of equal worth. Because most societies privilege men as a group, social movements are necessary to achieve equality between women and men, with the understanding that gender always intersects with other social hierarchies. (p. 7)

Not surprisingly, these attempts at unifying definitions each proved to be problematic. Promoting solidarity among women more often than not masked real differences—analytic and political differences (Delmar, 1986, p. 11). Even if one agrees, in some general way, that women are oppressed, there are sure to be disagreements over the meaning and explanation of women's oppression, the ways in which it is experienced, and its remedies. For example, some feminists believed the root of women's oppression was in patriarchy and that "participation in a heterosexual relationship carried with it inevitable exploitation" (Evans, 1997, p. 11). Others looked to economic macrostructures as the source of all oppression, including women's. And yet what seems to remain the bottom line for many feminists, even with these differing explanations, is "the central, and crucial, organizing principle that gendered difference is an essential part of any discussion of the social and symbolic world" (Evans, 1997, p. 9).

THEORY OR MOVEMENT?

Having laid out a view here of feminism as an inseparably theoretical and political project, it is important to understand the roots of that division in the first place. A review of the vast literature on feminism suggests a more dualistic way of understanding the concept: as a social-political movement or as theory. Marilyn Frye (2000) articulates this dichotomy well: On the one hand, "Feminism may be understood as *theory*—systems of concepts, propositions and analysis that describe and explain women's situations and experiences and support recommendations about how to improve them" (p. 195). On the other hand, "Feminism may also be understood as a kind of *social movement*, one that may generate and be aided by theory" (p. 195). Frye points out that if we define feminism as theory, then we "must immediately say that there are many feminisms—many feminist theories" (p. 195).

Maggie Humm (1992) tries to elide this dualism by bringing together ideas and actions, theory and politics. "The *feminisms* that constitute 'feminism'—from social reform and suffrage campaigns through to academic feminist theory—are not indistinct. A broad frame is needed to encompass political activism as well as theory" (p. 1). For her, "the first idea that is likely to occur in the course of any historical thinking about feminism is that feminism is a *social force*" (p. 1). Humm understands that feminist ideas and politics have their source "in all societies which divide the sexes into differing cultural, economic or political spheres, [and where] women are less valued than men" (p. 1). She further argues that feminism "depends on the premise that women can consciously and collectively change their social place" (p. 1). Hence, historical context produces ideas and ideas produce political action.

Yet the dualism persists and history seems to have placed greater emphasis on the characterization of feminism as a political movement. In fact, for many feminism was made synonymous with the women's movement: "So unquestioningly are feminism and a women's movement assumed to be co-terminous that histories of feminism are often written as histories of the women's movement" (Delmar, 1986, p. 13). Not everyone agrees with this identification, however; others have argued that "while Feminism has usually developed out of activist women's movements aimed at changing women's situations, not all such movements have styled themselves 'feminist'" (Andermahr et al., 1997, p. 239). Nevertheless, linking feminism with the women's movement as a narrative strategy has produced what has come to be known as the "wave theory" of feminism.

THE WAVE THEORY OF FEMINISM: AN OVERVIEW

Although it has become a commonplace to describe the history of feminism in terms of a first, second, and third wave, not all historians write the story this way.[2] As Barbara Caine (1997) reminds us, "Now . . . it is possible to construct a more or less continuous history of [British] feminism, showing its persistence in terms of published texts and active engagement at least from the seventeenth century to the present" (p. 1). Olive Banks (1981) also takes exception to the wave framework. She sees "the old and new feminism as one single historical process" (p. 1). And many of the new generation of feminists feel strongly that "second and third wave feminists are neither incompatible nor opposed" (Heywood & Drake, 1997, p. 3); that they are, in fact, a continuation in many ways of the work done before them.

Like these and other scholars, we find this taken-for-granted framework of three waves to be of limited value, and ask, as Linda Nicholson (1997) has, "What activities and what social groups are excluded by this distinction? What countries does it or does it not apply to?" (p. 1). And Kathyrn McPherson (2000, p. 210) reminds us that the most obvious limitation of this view of history is that it "masks the substantial feminist activism occurring before and after the ostensible 'crest'" and seems to assume that there will be an inevitable decline in feminist activity following that crest. It emphasizes discontinuities over continuities and neglects the fact that these "waves" are more like strands—not succeeding one another, but co-existing and often interweaving with one another. Finally, the danger of a "wave" theory, like a "stage" theory, is in suggesting some kind of progress. For all of these reasons we find this account problematic if taken too literally. Nevertheless, because these are the categories used in so many discussions of feminism, we provide a brief overview of the history of feminism viewed through this frame, acknowledging its weaknesses and limitations as well as its influence on the development of feminism's understanding of itself.

FIRST-WAVE FEMINISM

Feminism, like any social movement, did not develop in a vacuum. There were particular conditions that gave impetus to and nurtured it. Early feminists of the first wave were influenced by the prevailing ideologies of their era, including evangelical Christianity, Enlightenment philosophy, communitarian socialism, and maternal feminism, as well as the social and economic changes brought on by industrialization (McPherson, 2000, p. 208; Banks, 1981, pp. 7–8; Humm, 1992, p. 2). There is some discrepancy over the exact dates defining the parameters of the first wave. For example, McPherson (2000) marks the beginning of the first wave at 1880; Kemp and Squires (1997) post it at 1830; and Olive Banks (1981) refines it into "the early years," beginning at 1840, and "the golden years" from 1879 to 1920. Yet, we can say with some certainty that feminism as an organized movement gained momentum in the mid-nineteenth century in the United States and Britain with the involvement of (mostly middle-class white) women in the main social reform efforts of the day. The revivalism of evangelical movements fueled feminists with a missionary zeal and launched them into the public domain. It was through their work against slavery and for temperance that "women began to emerge from domesticity" (Banks, 1981, p. 7) and "challenge their exclusion from the public realm" (McPherson, 2000, p. 208). Their involvement in these social causes was buttressed by the "liberal rights perspective" promoted by such thinkers as John Stuart Mill, Harriet Taylor, and Mary Wollstonecraft.[3] Natural rights theory allowed women to begin to see "differences between men and women . . . as shaped by the environment rather than as natural" (Banks, 1981, p. 7). It

also raised awareness about the similarities between women's situation and that of other "oppressed" peoples, especially enslaved people (pp. 7–8).

Enlightenment philosophy also supported the possibility for "self-realization, freedom and autonomy" as well as for fundamental equality between persons—male or female, black or white (Banks, 1981, p. 8). This is not to say that all "enlightened" thinkers believed women were equal to men; in fact, "modern feminism has . . . come to be seen not as a simple outgrowth of the enlightenment . . . but rather a *consequence* of the new forms of discrimination which women faced at this time when they were explicitly denied rights being granted men" (Caine, 1997, p. 5, emphasis added). Juliet Mitchell grasped the power of such paradoxes for the formation of feminist consciousness in citing "the contradiction between the domestic ideology and women's productive role . . . between their role in the family and the work force, and . . . between the ideology of sexual freedom and women's actual sexual exploitation" (quoted in Banks, 1981, p. 6).

The other powerful intellectual and political influence on these early feminists was the communitarian socialism of the Saint Simonians (Banks, 1981, p. 8). This worldview offered a radical rethinking of family life, the role of women in child rearing, and sexual relations (p. 8). Women saw the possibilities for emancipation within their own homes. Marxist socialists also offered a critique of the family and advocated for a prominent role for the state in the everyday lives of women and children.

These distinct influences, although contradictory in many ways, expressed "the several faces of feminism" (Banks, 1981, p. 8) and supported a popular movement addressing women's social, economic, and political rights (McPherson, 2000, p. 208). One dimension of this evolving consciousness was "the recognition that women's social inferiority might be consequent upon their lack of education and opportunity, not a product of 'nature'" (Code, 2000, p. xxi). As Banks (1981, pp. 4–5) makes clear, "structural changes in society" were an important cause of the rise of feminism, especially for white middle-class women, who became increasingly dissatisfied with the constraints on their lives. As the "gap between men's and women's lives" expanded, especially in middle-class families, middle-class women, recognizing their unequal opportunities and conditions, began to speak out and organize. The identification of the feminist movement with white middle-class women, beginning with these early activists, affected the women's movement for decades and invited criticism for being "unrepresentative of the needs of women as a whole" (p. 5). Consequently, many second- and third-wave feminists have made it a priority to understand the intersection between sex/gender, class, and race (Heywood & Drake, 1997; Gillis, Howie, & Mumford, 2004; Walker, 1995).

The commitment to middle-class white issues deepened by 1900 when feminists made a pragmatic political decision to delimit their ideological differences and focus on the suffrage campaign (Banks, 1981, pp. 6–7; McPherson, 2000, pp. 208–209). Yet in doing so, feminism lost some of its radical edge (Banks, 1981, p. 84). One aspect of this tamer approach to women's issues was a basic transformation in how womanhood was conceived or constructed. No longer were feminists articulating the Enlightenment view of equality between men and women; many of them shifted to maternal feminism and its "notion of female superiority," which included "an acceptance of the *essential* uniqueness of the female" (Banks, 1981, p. 84, emphasis added), a theme that recurs in second-wave radical and cultural feminism. This maternal ideology served to legitimate women's "superior morality," especially that of white women, and was used to justify their "special 'civilising' role" (McPherson, 2000, p. 208). In this rhetoric of maternalism we see a preview of how contested the construction of womanhood would become and a glimpse of what later came to be known as the essentialism-antiessentialism debate.

After the vote was achieved (in 1920 in the United States and 1928 in Britain), and "despite sustained feminism internationally," the common historical record suggests that "the momentum of the 'first wave' had passed" (McPherson, 2000, p. 209). This did not deter some historians from noting a continuity between the first and second waves (Banks, 1981, pp. 153–154). For example, there remained a strong emphasis on legal achievements and on state and government reform as the locus of feminist efforts. Women's groups engaged in antipoverty activism and organized for international peace and freedom. And it was during this time (1923) that the Equal Rights Amendment was first written, thought it wasn't formally proposed in Congress until 1972 (Humm, 1992, p. 3).

SECOND-WAVE FEMINISM

Just as the social, economic, and political context of the nineteenth century gave rise to the first wave of feminism, so too did the particular historical circumstances of the early 1960s reinvigorate a second wave of modern feminism. By the early 1960s, demographic changes had transformed the labor force. Women, especially white middle-class women in the United States and Britain, postponed marriage, worked outside the home, had fewer children, divorced more, and sought higher education (Banks, 1981, pp. 210–211; Humm, 1992, p. 54). Although conventional "herstory" dates the start of second-wave feminism with the publication in 1963 of Betty Freidan's *The Feminine Mystique*, Banks argues that the story is more complex. She sees the book as "a *consequence* rather than a *cause* of a new mood among middle class women" (p. 211, emphasis added). (Here again, the standard account emphasizes the significance of social and political trends over theoretical influences.) Women were restless, unsatisfied with their treatment both in and out of the home. Consequently, they were "predisposed" to fight for equal rights again. The maternal feminism of the late first wave lost some of its power as women demanded to be treated as equals with men, rather than as distinctively different from (and in some ways better than) men.

The equal rights discourse of the 1960s and 1970s differed significantly from that of the first-wave equal rights movement, however. Although both generations of feminists fought for equality in the legal, educational, and economic spheres, "second wave feminism [took] as its starting point the politics of reproduction" (Humm, 1992, p. 53). Humm insists that "reproduction rights are to second wave feminists what production rights are to first wave feminists" (p. 53). This "fight for reproductive rights entails a fight against sexual and domestic violence and has profound repercussions for gender identity" (p. 54). So, issues of contraception, access to safe abortions, and sexual freedom rose to the fore. Humm argues that "the recognition that public policies could be crafted from private experience is unique to feminism. Indeed the single most important feature of feminism is its challenge to traditional political concepts" (p. 55). She elaborates by saying that "by connecting issues of reproduction to production, the personal with the political, second wave feminism changed contemporary political thinking" (p. 55). Nicholson (1997) echoes this sentiment when she observes that "the political movements that came into being in the 1960s meant a radical questioning of gender roles was being carried out not only by isolated scholars or marginalized groups but in front of and with the attention of many natural publics" (p. 1).

Some feminists suggest that two separate political movements were initiated at this time: "women's rights" feminism and the "women's liberation movement" (Nicholson, 1997, p. 1). The former, drawing on the dissatisfaction of white middle-class housewives, as portrayed by Freidan, had at its core professional women who fought to end workplace inequalities. The latter was a radical wing of the feminist movement that had felt excluded from leadership, decision making, and intellectual roles within both the civil rights movement and new left politics. These women took it upon themselves to form women-only "consciousness-raising groups" to better understand women's experience and the influence of patriarchy on their lives, individually and collectivity. "Patriarchy or women's oppression by man" (Banks, 1981, p. 227) was addressed as a more fundamental oppression than even the class inequalities of capitalism (Nicholson, 1997, p. 2). This ideological shift led to some painful divides within the larger left-wing political movements of the day, not only between men and women but also with equal rights feminists and to some extent with socialist feminists (Banks, 1981, p. 227).

Radical feminists developed a critical analysis of patriarchy and examined how "women and men, generally speaking, live[d] markedly different lives from one another, structurally, materially, experientially" (Code, 2000, p. xix). This attention to patriarchy required a new kind of theorizing; traditional liberal political theory and Marxist-socialist analysis were deemed insufficient. According to Nicholson (1997), although the women's rights movement, based on liberal principles of equality and freedom, was more prevalent in the United States, "it is from the Women's Liberation Movement that most theoretical works of the second wave have emerged" (p. 2). Understanding and eliminating systems of women's oppression became the focus of these radical feminists. Working with and against Marxist theory, they looked for ways to explain women's oppression. Some were more sympathetic to Marxist analysis and "tried to work out ways of theorizing the specificity and seriousness of women's oppression without discarding the insights of Marxism altogether" (p. 2).

With both radical and socialist feminists agreeing on the deficiencies of the liberal view that "women and men are the same," they developed new theoretical tools "that can be described as 'difference' feminism" (Nicholson, 1997, p. 3). However, this new theorizing about differences between men and women "suffered from one serious weakness: it tended to deny difference *among* women . . . [and] seemed too often to involve homogeneous visions of womanhood" (p. 3). Further, even when differences between women were discussed, it was usually done "in conjunction with assertions of commonalities . . . [and] not surprisingly, when a commonality in gender was assumed, it was described from the perspective of those of privilege" (p. 4).

Women of color, in particular, were uncomfortable with the critique of patriarchy because it obscured the differences of class and color between and among women. Implicitly, it obscured and normalized the "privilege" of the white women who were theorizing gender distinctions (Nicholson, 1997, p. 4). The Combahee River Collective, a group of black feminists, "was founded in 1974 explicitly to contest the presumptive power of white feminists to speak for universal women" (Humm, 1992, p. 133). In their 1977 declaration, "A Black Feminist Statement," this collective of black women asserted that they "need[ed] to rely principally on other black women for their liberation—that no other group besides themselves would be as consistent and committed to winning their freedom" (Alcoff, 2000, p. 263). In the 1980s, Patricia Hill Collins extended this critique in her groundbreaking work, *Black Feminist Thought: Knowledge, Consciousness and the Politics of Empowerment*. Collins (1990) analyzes "the tension between the suppression of Black women's ideas and our intellectual activism in the face of that suppression" (p. 6). Collins argues that "this historical suppression of Black women's ideas had a pronounced influence on feminist theory" (p. 7).

Subsequently, many white feminists agreed that there needed to be "exploration into the unarticulated premises that made the assertion of gender commonality possible even when differences were being asserted" (Nicholson, 1997, p. 4). This exploration "led to what became perhaps the major theoretical debate of the 1990s, around 'essentialism'" (p. 4). Natalie Stoljar (2000) suggests that "essentialism is often identified with a perspective that privileges a white, middle-class, heterosexual conception of womanness and excludes women of colour and women of different classes or sexualities from the political category 'woman'" (p. 177). Poststructuralism played an important role in the essentialism debate as well, particularly with "a critique of autonomous, preconstituted conceptions of the subject, and of theories of language that construed meaning in representational or essentialist terms" (Nicholson, 1997, p. 4). These challenges required many feminists to grapple with the problem of a feminist politics that included "subjectivity as discursively constructed and multiple in nature," while also recognizing that "the political meaning of feminism cannot be derived from any pre-given concept of 'womanhood' but must evolve as different political actors . . . struggle over how gender is understood" (pp. 4–5). Here, notice, the development of feminism as a social and political movement began to run up against, and explicitly take on, more overtly theoretical concerns.

THIRD-WAVE FEMINISM

The political effect of poststructuralist ideas did not faze a new generation of young women in the 1990s who began to define themselves with
and against the feminism that shaped them. Many were the daughters of
second-wave activists, with the benefits and baggage of that lineage. Once
again, historical context is crucial to understand the importance of this
stage of feminism. With a conservative shift in culture and politics, and
with the media proclaiming a "postfeminist" era,[4] in which many of the
concerns of previous feminists had presumably been remedied, or at least al-
leviated, these third-wave feminists were—and still are—creating a political
movement that has "been shaped by struggles between various feminisms
as well as by cultural backlash against feminism and activism" (Heywood
& Drake, 1997, p. 2). Many of these women understand themselves in
the tradition of second-wave feminism, but with a twist: "we define feminism's third wave as a movement that contains elements of second wave
critique of beauty, sexual abuse and power structures while it also acknowledges and makes use of the pleasure, danger, and defining power of those
structures" (p. 3). These grassroots activist-scholars developed political and
cultural practices around such themes as "Grrrl" power in order to expand
the boundaries of what it means to be a feminist. There is often an irony in
these activities, taking up elements of traditionally feminine preoccupations
(such as wearing makeup), but playing against those traditional manners
through performative and subversive reappropriations of them. At the same
time, by focusing on "psychiatric abuse, sexuality, harassment in schools, fat
activism, and cultural participation," third wavers also see "the centrality of
anger, used as a mechanism to provide voice to girls who had been silenced
in society and within feminism" (Starr, 2000, p. 474).

Third-wave feminists embody the contradictions of a generation who
"grew up with equity feminism, got gender feminism in college, along with
poststructuralism, and are now hard at work on a feminism that strategically
combines elements of these feminisms, along with black feminism, women-
of-color feminism, working-class feminism, pro-sex feminism, and so on"
(Heywood & Drake, 1997, p. 3). Committed to "a more racially and sexu-
ally diverse movement," these daughters of the second wave "emphasized
female empowerment rather than male oppression" (Freedman, 2002, p.
6). One of these feminists is Rebecca Walker, the daughter of second-wave
"womanist" Alice Walker. Rebecca, in declaring her identity, announced

"I'm not a post-feminist . . . I'm the Third Wave" (Freedman, 2002, p. 6). She and her colleagues of the third wave have resisted what they see as the conservative postfeminist analysis of the 1980s and are working to highlight and transform what they see as "the multiple, constantly shifting basis of oppression" (Heywood & Drake, 1997, p. 3). They, like many who grew up with the ideas of postmodern uncertainty, hybridity, and transgression, are more comfortable living in the in-between spaces of feminisms. As "products of all the contradictory definitions of and differences within feminism," they "make things 'messier' by *embracing* second wave critique . . . while emphasizing ways that desires and pleasures subject to critique can be used to rethink and enliven activist work" (pp. 3, 7).

These young women are more comfortable with the strategies of multicultural and cross-racial political activism. In fact, they look (back) to, and honor, the "third world feminism of the early 1980s" exemplified by the "landmark anthology *The Bridge Called My Back*" (Heywood & Drake, 1997, p. 8).[5] For many of these young women of the 1990s, third-wave feminism is forever indebted to third world theorizing. It was the critique of white Western feminism by women of color that inspired and fortified this new generation of feminists, as well as cautioning them to be mindful of (mis)appropriating that same critique (pp. 9–10).

As we have entered a new millennium, feminism has come to reflect "the cumulative contributions of working-class women, lesbians, women of color and activists from the developing world" (Freedman, 2002, p. 6). This more "mature feminist movement" acknowledges, and even embraces, contradictory positions with regard to race, class, gender, and other social categories (p. 6). At the same time, this new generation recognizes that what they imagine feminism to be may not be so easily attained (Spencer, 2004, p. 9). In Jane Spencer's (2004) genealogical account of third-wave feminism, she invokes Julia Kristeva to understand the challenges and complexities new feminists face with regard to identity and politics. And she reminds us that "there is no clear agreement as to what third wave feminism is even about" (p. 9). Spencer suggests that "to [the] extent that it is a generational phenomenon, [we need to address] . . . the question of what can or should be passed on from one set of feminists to the next, and to what extent the rising generation must rebel against the earlier" (pp. 9–10).

So we end this historical review by returning to our earlier concern with the problem of defining feminism during this more self-consciously eclectic and decentered time. Fortunately for our purposes here, we do not need so much to resolve the internal disputes of the various feminism(s) as to describe them clearly. (Nor do we think we could resolve them if we tried.) Our closest effort has been to characterize the acknowledgment of this ongoing internal conversation (or disputation) as itself partly constitutive of a distinctively feminist approach to social-political organization and action.

NOTES

1.   "Repositioning" has been borrowed from Jipson, Munro, Victor, Froude-Jones, and Freed-Rowland (1995).
2.   See Barbara Caine (1997); Olive Banks (1981); Heywood and Drake (1997).
3.   See J.S. Mill's (1869) *The Subjection of Women*, Harriet Taylor's (1851/1983) *The Enfranchisement of Women*, and Wollstonecraft's (1792) *A Vindication of the Rights of Woman*.
4.   *Postfeminism* is a contested term that connotes, on the one hand, a conservative media antifeminist moment, and on the other hand a new phase of feminism that "expresses the intersection of feminism with postmodernism, poststructuralism and postcolonialism" (Brooks, 1997, p. 4).
5.   See Anzaldua and Moraga (1983).

REFERENCES

Alcoff, L. (2000). Identity politics. In L. Code (Ed.), *Encyclopedia of feminist theories* (pp. 263–264). London: Routledge.

Andermahr, S., Lovell, T., & Wolkowitz, C. (1997). *A concise glossary of feminist theory*. London: Arnold.

Anzaldua, G., & Moraga, C. (Eds.). (1983). *This bridge called my back: Writings by radical women of color*. Latham, NY: Kitchen Table, Women of Color.

Banks, O. (1981). *Faces of feminism: A study of feminism as a social movement*. Oxford, UK: Martin Robertson.

Beasley, C. (1999). *What is feminism? An introduction to feminist theory*. London: Sage.

Brooks, A. (1997). *Postfeminism: Feminism, cultural theory and cultural forms*. London: Routledge.

Caine, B. (1997). *English feminism 1780–1980*. Oxford, UK: Oxford University Press.

Code, L. (Ed.). (2000). *Encyclopedia of feminist theories*. New York: Routledge.

Collins, P.H. (1990). *Black feminist thought: Knowledge, consciousness and the politics of empowerment*. Boston: Unwin Hyman.

Combahee River Collective. (2003). A black feminist statement. In C. McCann & S. Kim (Eds.), *Feminist theory reader: Local and global perspectives* (pp. 164–171). New York: Routledge.

Delmar, R. (1986). What is feminism? In J. Mitchell & A. Oakley (Eds.), *What is feminism?* (pp. 8–33). Oxford, UK: Basil Blackwell.

Evans, M. (1997). *Introducing contemporary feminist thought.* Cambridge, UK: Polity Press.

Freedman, E. (2002). *No turning back: The history of feminism and the future of women.* New York: Ballantine.

Frye, M. (2000). Feminism. In L. Code (Ed.), *Encyclopedia of feminist theories* (pp. 195–197). London: Routledge.

Gillis, S., Howie, G., & Mumford, R. (Eds.). (2004). *Third wave feminism: A critical exploration.* New York: Palgrave Macmillan.

Heywood, L., & Drake, J. (Eds.). (1997). *Third wave agenda: Being feminist, doing feminism.* Minneapolis: University of Minnesota Press.

hooks, b. (1984). *Feminist theory from margin to center.* Boston: South End Press.

hooks, b. (2003). Feminism: A movement to end sexist oppression. In C. McCann & S. Kim (Eds.), *Feminist theory reader: Local and global perspectives* (pp. 50–56). New York: Routledge.

Hughes, C. (2002). *Key concepts in feminist theory and research.* London: Sage.

Humm, M. (Ed.). (1992). *Feminisms: A reader.* Hertfordshire, UK: Harvester Wheatsheaf. (Also published in 1992 as *Modern feminisms: Political, literary, cultural.* New York: Columbia University Press.)

Jaggar, A. (Ed.). (1994). *Living with contradictions: Controversies in feminist social ethics.* Boulder, CO: Westview.

Jipson, J., Munro, P., Victor, S., Froude-Jones, K., & Freed-Rowland, G. (1995). *Repositioning feminism and education: Perspectives on educating for social change.* Westport, CT: Bergin and Garvey.

Kemp, S., & Squires, J. (Eds.). (1997). *Feminisms.* Oxford, UK: Oxford University Press.

Lather, P. (2007). *Getting lost: Feminist efforts toward a double(d) science.* Albany: State University of New York Press.

McPherson, K. (2000). First-wave/second-wave feminism. In L. Code (Ed.), *Encyclopedia of feminist theories* (pp. 208–210). London: Routledge.

Mill, J.S. (1869). *The subjection of women.* New York: D. Appelton.

Mitchell, J., & Oakley, A. (Eds.). (1986). *What is feminism?* Oxford, UK: Basil Blackwell.

Nicholson, L. (Ed.). (1997). *The second wave: A reader in feminist theory.* New York: Routledge.

Olesen, V. (2005). Early millennial feminist qualitative research: Challenges and contours. In N. Denzin & Y. Lincoln (Eds.), *The Sage handbook of qualitative research* (3rd ed., pp. 235–278). Thousand Oaks, CA: Sage.

Spencer, J. (2004). Introduction: Genealogies. In S. Gillis, G. Howie, & R. Mumford (Eds.), *Third wave feminism: A critical exploration* (pp. 9–12). New York: Palgrave Macmillan.

Starr, C. (2000). Third-wave feminism. In L. Code (Ed.), *Encyclopedia of feminist theories* (pp. 474). London: Routledge.

Stoljar, N. (2000). Essentialism. In L. Code (Ed.), *Encyclopedia of feminist theories* (pp. 177–178). London: Routledge.

Taylor, H. (1983). *Enfranchisement of women.* London: Virago. (Original work published 1851).

Walker, R. (1995). *To be real: Telling the truth and changing the face of feminism.* New York: Anchor.

Wollstonecraft, M. (1792). *A vindication of the rights of woman.* London: J. Johnson.

CHAPTER 3

Philosophical Concerns and Commitments

FOLLOWING THE PREVIOUS CHAPTER'S OVERVIEW OF TRANSFORMATIONS in feminist history, here we turn our attention more specifically to the philosophical and theoretical commitments that have particular relevance for feminist research, especially research in education. We have argued that changes in feminism over time always have the dual aspects of changes to feminism as a social and political movement as well as changes to feminist theory—and these need to be seen in relation to each other. In this chapter our focus is more on the latter aspect: the epistemological and ontological debates that have shaped feminist theory, inquiry, and activism.

To do this, we look to the work of feminist philosophers who, over the past four decades, have challenged the "subtle underlying metaphysical and epistemological assumptions of our culture and our philosophical tradi-tions" (Garry & Pearsall, 1989, p. xi). As some of the strongest and most influential voices to emerge from second-wave feminist academic thought, these groundbreaking philosophers led the way in articulating a "range of different approaches, perspectives and frameworks that together constitute feminist philosophy" in order to understand, to explain, and ultimately to end the oppressive condition of women (Tuana & Tong, 1995, p. 3).

Feminism has a decidedly political agenda: liberating women. Hence it is often viewed primarily as a kind of political philosophy.[1] But political philosophy was not the only domain that received feminist treatment: no dimension of traditional philosophizing was exempt. Ethics, epistemology, metaphysics—even philosophical method itself—all proved fertile ground for feminist philosophers to rework.[2] At the risk of sounding tautological (and reductionist), the most fundamental commitment shared by the variety of feminist philosophers is that all are feminists: scholars who "seek to understand and explain women's experiences and women's practices . . . see women's subordination as systematic and structural; [and who] work toward the liberation of women" (Garry & Pearsall, 1989, p. xiii).

These early feminist philosophers saw themselves generating a counterdiscourse, or "reverse discourse" (Weiner, 1995, p. 64), to traditional mainstream philosophy—to what many saw as its "androcentric character" (Garry & Pearsall, 1989, p. xi). What does that actually mean? For Alison Jaggar, one of the leading feminist philosophers of this generation, it meant simply "a distinctively masculine way of approaching the world" (quoted in Tuana & Tong, 1995, p. 1). Lorraine Code (2000) defines androcentrism as "entrenched practices that base theory and practice on men's experiences masquerading as 'human' experiences and counting as unquestioned sources of knowledge 'in general'" (p. 20). For these feminist critics, mainstream or "malestream" philosophy was "limited, biased and liable to oppressive use" (Garry & Pearsall, 1989, p. xi). The counterdiscourse they developed reminded the world that "the adult white male can no longer be taken to represent all of humanity, nor the adult white male experience to encompass all that is important in human life" (Jaggar, 1988, p. 22). In part, these women's intellectual challenge to the academic discipline of philosophy resulted from their experience as graduate students and young scholars who were being initiated into a "privileged white male project" (Cole, 1993, p. 12). As emerging scholars, they felt firsthand these exclusions in theory and in lived practice.

By challenging "the central presuppositions and key concepts of the discipline," feminist philosophers set out to "reconstruct philosophy . . . in ways that value women's experiences and enable women to move from the position of object to positions of subject, of knower, and of agent" (Garry & Pearsall, 1989, p. xii). In their critique of the discipline of philosophy, feminists not only found an absence of women's experience, but also saw that "the concrete, particular and subjective . . . [were] viewed as the enemies of the abstract, universal and objective" (Tuana & Tong, 1995, p. 2). With their privileging of women's experience, feminist philosophers also went against the grain by announcing their commitment to an explicitly political project: liberating women from systematic oppression. This "philosophy of liberation" was a direct attack on the disinterested, neutral approach of most philosophy, particularly the Anglo-American analytic strands (Garry & Pearsall, 1989, p. xiii). As Eve Browning Cole (1993) reminds us, unlike Aristotle, "feminist philosophy begins, not in wonder, but in an intense political engagement"; it is "a direct response to real social movements and political problems" (p. 1).

Giving attention to women's experience demonstrates that gender matters; that in contrast to traditional (presumably but not exclusively male) philosophers, we must "resist easy moves to speak in a 'neutral,' nongendered voice" (Garry & Pearsall, 1989, p. xiii). Paying attention to gender means noticing how "the construction and elaboration of theoretical frameworks [has been affected by our social arrangements] including the sex/gender arrangements, within which knowledge is developed" (Nelson, 1990, p. 29). In this way, feminist philosophers are committed to examining the political and social construction of knowledge and the process of knowing. Contrary to the Anglo-analytic tradition, feminists see the sociohistorical context in which knowledge is produced as central to formulating their accounts of human experience.

In this critique, feminist scholars also attend to "who and what are being excluded from the domain of philosophical discourse, and for what reasons" (Cole, 1993, p. 13). Feminists such as Lynn Nelson (1990) articulate the need to highlight the overlooked experiences and practices of women, arguing that "our theories will be empirically sound only if they reflect, derive from, and are capable of explaining human experience" (p. 30). Furthermore, feminists felt that these exclusions and erasures not only "led to distortion and bias in philosophy itself" but actually contributed "to the oppression of women and other subordinate groups" (Garry & Pearsall, 1989, p. xi). That is why, for these scholars, philosophy is not merely academic; the ramifications are serious, affecting the lived reality of many. Here again, theoretical and practical and political concerns coincide.

In naming the exclusionary tendencies of androcentric philosophy, however, most feminist critics are not claiming that those traditionally excluded areas of human life "are inherently 'female' or 'feminine'"; but they would insist, as Alison Jaggar does, that they are symbolically coded by gender. For example, it is a cultural stereotype that "women are associated with the emotions and the body, whereas men are associated with reason and the mind" (Tuana & Tong, 1995, p. 2). This distinction regarding "inherent femaleness" suggests that many feminist philosophers recognized early on the difficulty in defining women's experience and what it means to be a "woman." Social constructivism as well as poststructuralist thought have assisted feminists in articulating the problem of womanhood, a problem that is often situated within the "essentialism-antiessentialism" debate.

To avoid, or correct, the perceived elitism and exclusive tendencies of traditional philosophy, feminist philosophers offered up some "general ground rules" for doing philosophy that included contextualizing or historicizing any theoretical or empirical inquiry; claiming experience, emotions, and perceptions as valid sources of knowledge claims; going beyond the traditional boundaries of philosophy for explanatory insight; and taking into account the social and political implications of philosophical inquiry (Cole, 1993, pp. 14–17). Many feminists argued that theories, "both longstanding and current, require substantial revision or need to be replaced by more adequate frameworks . . . to adequately account for *human* experience" (Nelson, 1990, pp. 29–30). As Sandra Harding (1986) makes clear, "what we took to be humanly inclusive problematics, concepts, theories, objective methodologies and transcendental truths are in fact less than that. Instead, these products of thought bear the mark of their collective and individual creators, and the creators in turn have been distinctively marked as to gender, class, race, and culture" (p. 15).

Feminist philosophy, therefore, offered a direct attack on three foundational pillars supporting mainstream philosophy: objectivity, neutrality, and impartiality (Garry & Pearsall, 1989, p. 1). This philosophical critique coincided with similar work being done within the natural and social sciences more generally; in fact, it became clear to many feminist scholars at the time that "eliminating sexist bias in biology and the social sciences might [also] require redefining objectivity, rationality, and scientific method" (Harding, 1991, p. 19). The feminist critique of science included a fundamental challenge, which has come to be known as "the 'science question' in feminism" (Harding, 1986). As Harding (1986) puts it, "Is it possible to use for emancipatory ends sciences that are apparently so intimately involved in Western, bourgeois, and masculine projects?" (p. 9).

In questioning the sexism of scientific research, feminist philosophers asked themselves, "perhaps the fundamental problem was epistemological" (Harding, 1991, p. 19). It is with this dimension of feminism that we enter an epistemological terrain that has been significant for a revisioning of philosophy and, by extension, social and scientific inquiry more gener-ally—including educational research. We review these arguments in some detail, not only for their own sake but because, as we will see, they play out in terms of specific practices, strategies, and values in the doing of research.

FEMINIST VIEWS ON EPISTEMOLOGY

One result of the intersection between feminism and philosophy was the attempt to develop "distinctively feminist theories of knowledge" (Harding, 1991, p. 105) that would contribute to what Harding (1986) names "'suc-cessor science' projects [that] aim to reconstruct the original goals of modern science" (p. 142). Since there was really no way of getting completely outside of "the received epistemologies of Anglo-American philosophy," many who were engaged in this endeavor worked "both within and in opposition" to them (Code, 1998, p. 175). Just as epistemology is not a monolithic field, there is no single unified notion of feminist epistemology: feminist philoso-phers coming from a range of different positions "engaged in a dialogue with one or more traditions in the history of epistemology" (Alcoff & Pot-ter, 1993, p. 2). This dialogue produced multiple epistemologies, exploring a range of issues "variously [called] 'women's ways of knowing,' 'women's experience,' or simply 'women's knowledge'" (Alcoff & Potter, 1993, p. 1).

As feminists "were reshaping epistemological inquiry" (Code, 1998, p. 176), they anticipated the possible reception to "the very idea of a feminist epistemology" (Nelson, 1999, p. 167). Some knew it would be seen as a "contradiction in terms" (Harding, 1991, p. 106) or an "oxymoron" (Alcoff & Potter, 1993, p. 1), or simply "incongruous on its face" (Nelson, 1999, p. 169), given the dominant view of epistemology that permeates contempo-rary philosophy.[3] Yet regardless of this predicted reception, feminist philos-ophers proceeded on the uncertain path of undermining the epistemological assumptions in which they had all been trained and remained immersed. Donna Haraway (1991) pondered the potential for feminist epistemology when she asked,

Do feminists have anything distinctive to say about the natural sciences? Should feminists concentrate on criticizing sexist science and the conditions of its production? Or should feminists be laying the foundation for an epistemological revolution illuminating all facets of scientific knowledge? . . .

Would feminist standards of knowledge genuinely end the di-
lemma of the cleavage between subject and object or between non-
invasive knowing and prediction and control? Does feminism offer
insight into the connections between science and humanism? Do
feminists have anything new to say about the vexed relations of
knowledge and power? Would feminist authority and the power
to name give the world a new identity, a new story? Can feminists
master science? (pp. 71–72)

These questions go to the heart of the limits and possibilities of developing a specifically feminist theory of knowledge. However, before we explore
these questions and delineate the range of answers feminists have offered,
we want to rehearse the conventional or received view of epistemology.[4]

Epistemology, historically thought to be the "core of philosophy" by
many (Garry & Pearsall, 1989, p. 109) "is that branch of philosophy which
is concerned with the nature and scope of knowledge, its presuppositions
and basis, and the general reliability of claims to knowledge."[5] According to
Lorraine Code (1998), "Mainstream Anglo-American epistemology had defined itself around a conviction that its principal task was to determine the
necessary and sufficient conditions for objective, uniformly valid 'knowledge in general'" (p. 173). This ostensibly general knowledge of human
experience was derived, by and large, by men, about men, and from male
experience. Women were not part of the equation.

Traditionally, epistemologists divided their focus into two domains: the
context of discovery and the context of justification. The former refers to
generating theories and hypotheses and the latter to testing them (Nelson,
1990, p. 46). As Phillips and Burbules (2000) put it, the "so-called . . .
context of discovery is the context in which discoveries in science are first
made, and the [so-called] context of justification is the context in which
these discoveries are justified or warranted as indeed being valid discoveries"
(p. 12). To them, "the distinction is sometimes useful as a crude tool but in
fact oversimplifies matters; discovery and justificatory processes take place
together and cannot be meaningfully separated—a researcher is always evaluating data, evaluating his or her procedures, deciding what to keep and
what to abandon, and so forth. In short, discovery and justification rarely
occur sequentially" (p. 12). However, most mainstream philosophers main-
tain that the context of discovery is "of no epistemological consequence"
(Nelson, 1990, p. 47), because where theories or hypotheses come from

does not matter to their truth; instead, they tended to focus on the context of justification.

Feminists offer a strong critique of this conceptual distinction. They argue that there are "blinders imposed by the philosophical distinction [and that] a theory of scientific inquiry that focuses solely on the logic of justification neglects the selection process occurring in the context of discovery that limit what we get to know about" (Longino, 1993b, p. 101). Furthermore, they insist that both contextual levels are crucial in doing their own work. Given that theories and hypotheses, historically, were generated in a context that excluded women and women's experience, feminists argued that the conditions under which theories and hypotheses were formed is in need of critical analysis. This critique connects to the feminist disavowal of the abstract, universal knower whose social and cultural location is irrelevant to how they come to know the world. Feminists believe that how we conceptualize ideas, and what we choose to focus on, are affected by our identity, subjectivity, and social location—hence the context of discovery is an important part of any line of inquiry.

Nevertheless, feminists also place primary emphasis on the issue of how we justify our claims and "what we mean when we say that a claim is true" (Alcoff, 1998, p. viii). A thumbnail account of modern Western epistemology divides it into three received traditions with different relations to knowledge and knowing: rationalism, empiricism, and naturalism. Descartes is credited with the epistemological legacy of rationalism, in which "the paradigm case of a knowledge situation is one in which purely conceptual entities are investigated by an equally pure mind unfettered by sense perceptions" (Cole, 1993, p. 73). In the quest for certainty, Descartes and generations of rationalists to follow "emphasized the need to justify our beliefs through tests of reason, logic, and clarity" (Alcoff, 1998, p. 3). It was by employing this rigorous standard of reason that rationalists sought to "provide secure foundations for human knowledge" (Gatens, 1998, p. 21). Some argue that "Descartes' [foundationalist] epistemological agenda has been the agenda of Western epistemology to this day" (Kim, 1998, p. 266). As we discuss later, this rationalist legacy has received substantial feminist criticism in recent years, particularly for its problematic valorization of "the man of reason" (Lloyd, 1993).

Empiricists such as Hume and Locke agreed with Descartes in his quest for certainty and foundational knowledge; however, they did not think that reason was an adequate source of knowledge. They argued that experience and the senses must be employed to know the world, using reason to help us. For Locke, "our ideas *originate* in experience . . . and . . . our ideas or knowledge claims have to be *justified or warranted* in terms of experience" (Phillips & Burbules, 2000, p. 7). Empiricists think that "careful and thorough observation, by a sufficiently open-minded knower, will eventually produce knowledge" (Cole, 1993, p. 76). This empirical method of knowing is, "at its core . . . a theory of evidence" (Nelson, 1998, p. 31). With "its emphasis . . . on neutral, replicable observation and experimental verification [and its] claim to offer the most purely objective route to knowledge of the 'external world'" (Code, 2000, p. 165), empiricism has become central to modern scientific inquiry.

Naturalized epistemology constitutes the third category of knowledge theories. In its pure form, à la Quine, "epistemology should be based, not on ideal abstract conditions, or on how we *think* we know based merely on introspection, but on the real processes of human perceiving and knowing" (Alcoff, 1998, p. 251). As Quine (1998) himself says, "Epistemology, or something like it, simply falls into place as a chapter of psychology and hence of natural science. It studies a natural phenomenon, viz., a physical human subject" (p. 260; Nelson, 1990, p. 278). Quine argued that "epistemology could find its answers by simply studying how believers actually justify their beliefs" (Alcoff, 1998, p. ix).

Many have interpreted Quine to mean that the "normative character" of epistemology is suspect and that cognitive science should become a resource for philosophers (Duran, 1991, p. 4). According to Jaegwon Kim (1998), Quine "is asking us to set aside the entire framework of justification-centered epistemology . . . to put in its place a purely descriptive, causal-nomological science of human cognition" (p. 271). However, there are many contemporary philosophers who disagree with this interpretation of Quine's intent. They argue that you can "expand the significance of psychological processes and social context for epistemology without replacing normative concerns with mere description" (Alcoff, 1998, p. 251). Some feminists have taken up naturalized epistemology as a view of knowledge "that promises enormous aid and comfort to feminists" (Antony, 1993, p. 187).

FEMINIST CRITIQUES OF THE RECEIVED TRADITIONS

Although decidedly different, these three epistemological positions each has received critical feminist treatment. A common criticism is that all three approaches depend upon the idea of "objective knowers [who] are disinterested in and separate from objects of knowledge. Knowledge emerges from, and serves, no specific interests or agendas" (Code, 2000, p. 367). Ideally, for this presumably "objective" pursuit of knowledge, the "observer [must be] completely free of clouding and coloring prejudice, preconception, emotion, perceptual impairment of any kind" (Cole, 1993, p. 77). Clearly, this contradicts the position held by a significant number of feminist philosophers who are not only open to and motivated by their interests and agendas, but disavow the possibility (or even the desirability) of disinterested knowledge. Lynn Nelson (1990) reminds us that "advocacy, involvement, and engagement are standardly taken to impair or preclude objectivity . . . [yet] there have been those like Marx and contemporary feminists who have maintained that political advocacy or position could provide an epistemological advantage" (p. 33).

Sandra Harding (1991) goes even further when she asks skeptically (and rhetorically), "can there be 'disinterested knowledge' in a society that is deeply stratified by gender, race, and class?" (pp. 109–110). The following litany of queries suggests her lack of faith in traditional epistemology: "who can be subjects, agents, of socially legitimate knowledge? (Only men in the dominant races and classes?) . . . what kind of tests must beliefs pass in order to be legitimated as knowledge? (Only tests against the dominant group's experiences and observations?) . . . what is the nature of objectivity? Does it require 'point-of-viewlessness'?" (p. 109).

For Harding and other feminist critics, these questions go to the core of the views on knowledge that have influenced so much of what counts as modern science (Lather, 1991, p. 104). Feminists are casting doubt on what has come to be known as "the view from nowhere," wondering who is capable of such a view (Code, 2000, p. 170), and whether, even if it were possible, it would be desirable. Donna Haraway, in her provocative classic essay "Situated Knowledges," suggests that this "fiction of objectivity" is possible only by those "performing a 'god-trick'" (Code, 2000, p. 170; Haraway, 1991, p. 193). She is referring to "those occupying the positions of dominators" (Haraway, 1991, p. 193). In Haraway's incisive critique, contrary to the hegemonic view of positivism, the position of dominators— "the standpoint of the master, the Man [is] the only position from which objectivity *could not possibly* be practiced and honored" (p. 193, emphasis added). Similarly, in *Feminist Politics and Human Nature*, Allison Jaggar (1988) argues for a different understanding of objectivity and universality.

Referring to the "post-Newtonian conception" of science, Jaggar (1988) insists that "the scientist can no longer be seen as a detached observer whose values are irrelevant to his or her science but rather must be acknowledged as a 'participator' whose science reflects his or her values" (p. 368).

Phillips and Burbules (2000) do not disagree. In fact, they argue that "every inquirer *must* adopt a framework or perspective or point of view" (p. 46). And they agree with the need to expand the scientific community to include more diverse perspectives on research matters. In this way, they are sympathetic to some aspects of the feminist critique of epistemology and science. However, they are less persuaded by the charge of androcentrism that indicts "the categories and conceptual tools of science [as] male biased" (p. 50). They insist that, as intriguing as that criticism is, "it is an impossible charge to substantiate if inquiry is necessarily always subverted" (p. 51).

So, what are feminist epistemologists seeking? Most want to develop the means to gather more complete evidence, to warrant more inclusive, more accurate, more accountable descriptions and explanations of the world—natural and social.[6] Helen Longino (1993b) says it powerfully: "Feminists, faced with traditions in philosophy and in science that are deeply hostile to women, have had practically to invent new and more appropriate ways of knowing the world. These new ways have been less invention out of whole cloth than the revival or reevaluation of alternative or suppressed traditions" (p. 101). For example, Nobel Prize winner Barbara McClintock is often cited by feminists for her "loving identification with various aspects of the plants she studied," which she claimed actually improved the scientific quality of her research (Longino, 1993b, p. 101). Yet this same behavior was partly why her male colleagues marginalized her and undermined her "epistemic authority" (Code, 1998, p. 176).

The lived reality of women affected how feminist philosophers came to understand knowledge and inquiry. Unlike their male colleagues who embraced the idealized, abstract, interchangeable knower, feminists knew—intuitively, experientially, and from critical analysis—that it was important "to ground their normative conclusions in the epistemic demands that real, embodied, specifically located knowers face" (Code, 1998, p. 176). Also unlike most of their male counterparts, feminists acknowledged a vested interest in their inquiries—whether in the natural or social sciences. They argued that having an open interest in what they researched (as opposed to the purported disinterest of traditional research) does not necessarily produce biased or distorted knowledge. In fact, they insist that because of systematic sexism in institutions, and because of the prevalent androcentrism of scientific thinking, such purported disinterest actually itself creates biases and blind spots; hence there needs to be an explicit commitment to remedy the situation. Without this intention to correct pervasively gender-biased methods and analyses, science will keep producing inadequate, incomplete, unwarranted, and biased accounts of the world.

It is the contradiction between the espoused objectivity and value neutrality of the traditional researcher, and what feminists saw as the biased, distorted knowledge produced from that approach, that propelled many of them to reconceptualize the research process. Feminist scholars insisted that by incorporating the perspective of women's lives, they would produce a more objective, more complete view of the world than the limited one produced from the traditional, elite circle of white middle-class researchers. There was common agreement among feminists on the political nature of feminism and its commitment to social change (Harding, 1986, p. 24). Thus the question for them was, "How can such politicized research be increasing the objectivity of inquiry? On what grounds should these feminist claims be justified?" (p. 24).

Although most feminists agree on the general critique of philosophy and science as exclusionary and biased, not all feminists agree on the same remedy, however. Just as with feminism in general, where there are multiple perspectives, so too are there different strands of feminist epistemology, with different assumptions about knowledge and with different implications for research and inquiry. We address three distinct perspectives within feminist epistemology: feminist empiricism; feminist standpoint/feminist materialist theory; and feminist postmodernism/poststructuralism. Although this tripartite "taxonomy," first presented by Sandra Harding in *The Science Question in Feminism* is a bit dated (not unlike the wave theory of feminism), it will serve for our purposes here, as a convenient heuristic to understand some trends in feminist epistemology (Harding, 1986, p. 24; Code, 1998, p. 176).

FEMINIST EMPIRICISM

Feminist empiricists, named initially by Sandra Harding to distinguish their position from her notion of feminist standpoint theory, appear to have the most faith of all feminists in the conventional theory of knowledge and its relation to scientific inquiry. They start with "the contention that feminists—

like other would-be-knowers—have to base their knowledge on *empirical evidence*" (Code, 1998, p. 176, emphasis added). Harding called the early feminist empiricist writing of the early 1970s and 1980s "'spontaneous' feminist empiricist epistemology" because it "arose as the 'spontaneous consciousness' of feminist researchers in biology and the social sciences who were trying to explain what was and what wasn't different about their research process" (Harding, 1993, p. 51).

Like many other feminist philosophers, feminist empiricists criticized traditional epistemology, especially its sexism and androcentrism, and the accompanying "fiction of knowers as detached and neutral information-processors" (Code, 1998, pp. 176–177). For Helen Longino, "scientific inquiry cannot be value-free, as traditional empiricists required, for cultural and social values make knowledge possible" (Code, 1998, p. 178). Feminist empiricists, in "reject[ing] the presumed value-neutrality of science . . . show how values are inevitably employed in the justification of theories" (Tanesini, 1999, p. 97). Feminist empiricists also "acknowledge[d] that science is a human social activity and that it would be a mistake to reduce scientific practice to the theories it produces" (p. 97). With this acknowledgment, "they realize that any adequate account of knowledge would have to consider its social dimension . . . an aspect of science that had been ignored by old-style empiricism" (p. 97). Longino (1990) was one of the pioneers of this notion of "contextual empiricism" (p. 185).

Yet, feminist empiricists believed, unlike feminist standpoint theorists, for example, that "sexist and androcentric biases can be eliminated by *stricter adherence* to existing methodological norms of scientific inquiry" (Harding, 1991, p. 111, emphasis added; also see Harding, 1993, p. 51; Harding, 1986, p. 24). The same feminists felt that, with the increased opportunities for women to become scientists, there was a better chance to eliminate sexist biases in the research process. They believed that women scientists "are more likely than men to notice androcentric bias" and that feminists "*as a group* are more likely to produce unbiased and objective results than are men (or nonfeminists) as a group" (Harding, 1986, p. 25).

Feminist empiricism took the notion of experiential knowledge very seriously, attending to the embedded, embodied particularities of experience, and of the knower. This led to problematizing the idea of neutral inquiry and promoting the idea "that an unabashedly value-laden yet rigorous empiricism can produce more adequate knowledge than an empiricism whose practitioners are ignorant of the effects of their own specificity and of their complicity in sustaining systems of asymmetrical epistemic power and privilege" (Code, 1998, p. 177). Similar to Sandra Harding's (1991, p. 138) concept of "strong objectivity," feminist empiricists suggest that "politically informed inquiry fosters a *better* empiricism, and generates a stronger, more rigorous objectivity" than the traditional notion of objective research (Code, 1998, p. 177, emphasis added). Yet, as Harding (1986) points out, this reliance on "the social identity of the inquirer" poses a major paradox or challenge for feminist empiricists, given that in traditional empiricism, the identity of the inquirer should be "irrelevant to the 'goodness' of the results of the research" (p. 25).

Feminist empiricism, particularly the "neo-empiricist feminist epistemologies of the 1990s" (Code, 1998, p. 178), undermines another institutionalized practice within traditional empiricist research, the construction of the knower as individual (Longino, 1993b, p. 104). Instead, Helen Longino, Lynn Nelson, Jane Duran, and others stress "the move toward community-located theories of knowledge" (Code, 1998, p. 178). Longino argues that "scientific knowledge is constructed not by individuals applying a method to the material to be known but by individuals in interaction with one another" (Longino, 1993b, p. 111). This "pluralistic conception of inquiry" (Code, 1998, p. 178), or "contextual empiricism" (Tanesini, 1999, p. 98), advocates for a different approach to doing science that "includes more than just the complex of activities that constitutes hypothesis testing through comparison of hypothesis statements with . . . experiential data" (Longino, 1993b, p. 111). Longino insists that "conceptual and evidential scrutiny and criticism" should be applied equally to the researcher's "background assumptions" as well as other data and hypotheses (p. 111), because these "background assumptions play a constitutive part in knowledge acquisition and evaluation" (Code, 1998, p. 178). She also insists that it is crucial to analyze the relationship between these background assumptions and the "evidential reasoning" of the researcher (Longino, 1993a, p. 263). Longino's empiricism places a strong emphasis on how these background assumptions are influenced by "social values and ideology," and so there must be "criteria for ruling out, limiting, or selecting background assumptions" (p. 263).

Disrupting the assumptions of the scientific community, Longino wants to make visible who belongs to this community and what values and views they bring to the endeavor. To do so, Longino (1993b) argues for a research process that incorporates "alternative points of view" from knowers outside of the scientific community, who can provide "effective criticism of background assumptions" (p. 112). A significant "outcome of [this] critical dialogue" is knowledge "constructed not by individuals but by an interactive dialogic community" (Longino, 1993b, p. 112). Developed from feminist principles, this contextualized empirical inquiry produces an "objectivity . . . [that] is an explicitly communicative, communal achievement" (Code, 1998, p. 178).

Longino (1993a) argues that the contextualism she is promoting "does not demand relativism; rather, it demands a fuller account of objectivity and knowledge from which normativity can be generated" (p. 263). Unlike traditional empirical science, Longino believes that it is impossible to rid the inquiry process of "ideological and value issues" (p. 270). She insists, "What is important is not that they be banished, but that we have (1) analytic tools that enable us to identify them, and (2) community practices that can (in the long run) regulate their role in the development of knowledge" (p. 270). This is why Longino insists that "the practices of inquiry are not individual but social" (p. 263). Longino also maintains that both the context of discovery and the context of justification must be "open to rigorous critique" because "the value-laden assumptions go much deeper, shaping the conceptualization of projects, the hypotheses that guide and regulate inquiry, and the taken-for-granted beliefs about what counts as evidence and what amounts merely to an aberration" (Code, 1998, p. 178). Concurring with other feminists, Longino stresses the import of what seems self-evident to them but is not assumed by traditional researchers: "that diverse background assumptions can produce radically different readings of 'the same' natural phenomena" (Code, 1998, p. 178). We need not only a "community of inquiry" but a diverse one; and constraints upon that diversity are themselves constraints on the adequacy of their truth claims.

Lynn Nelson's "naturalized empiricism" (Tanesini, 1999, p. 101) similarly argues against the individualism of traditional epistemology. Nelson (1993) assumes that "the agents of feminist epistemologies, of sociology of knowledge, and of some empiricist frameworks, differ significantly from the abstract (context-independent and disembodied) 'individuals' of foundationalist epistemologies" (p. 121). She goes on to argue, "'The Knower' of the frameworks developed by Descartes, Hume and the early and later formulations of positivism was basically passive, a recipient or collector of knowledge" (p. 121). Inspired by Quine's naturalized epistemology, Nelson "rethinks the whole idea of evidence within a conception of knowers as collaborative agents, whose epistemic projects are shaped by, and require evaluation within, the communities where their knowledge-producing practices occur" (Code, 1998, pp. 178–179). Nelson (1993) is not denying "that individuals know," but rather that "the knowing we do as individuals is derivative, that your knowing and mine depends on *our* knowing" (p. 124).

Lorraine Code (1998) reminds us that in her "robust version of empiricism" Nelson sees "the radical potential of Quinean epistemology" (p. 179). Nelson "is respectful of evidence and of the impressive achievements of the natural sciences, yet resistant to representing items of knowledge as discrete or autonomous, isolated from the 'webs of belief' that contain and make them possible" (Code, 1998, p. 179). Nelson's feminist naturalized epistemology extends Quine's commitment to understanding how people come to know; how we construct our knowledge based on the interaction of our beliefs, evidence, and theoretical possibilities. Where she goes beyond Quine is in her insistence on exposing "the gender, race, and class insensitivities carried within the going theories of social science, including the very scientific psychology which for Quine, becomes the place where epistemology is made" (Code, 1998, p. 179).

Another important feminist epistemologist who remains loyal to the empiricist tradition is Jane Duran. She too, like Nelson, is aligned with Quine's naturalized epistemology and "treats knowledge as communally acquired, corroborated, and elaborated" (Code, 1998, p. 179). Less committed to the sociocultural critique of Nelson and Longino, Duran attempts to stay within the analytic tradition. She maintains that "however androcentric the tradition of the professional epistemologists had been . . . it has the virtue of being a rigorous method of inquiry" (Duran, 1991, p. 15). Duran accompanies this praise of the analytic tradition with a critique of feminist epistemology: "it is not so rigorous, not so specific, nor so finely tuned" (p. 15). Wanting to incorporate what she understands "as essentially feminine principles and modes of reasoning," Duran developed an approach or model with "empirical-analytic rigor" that "draw[s] on object-relations theory, psychoanalysis, and cognitive science to examine how male and female knowers are psychologically produced and reproduced" (Code, 1998, p. 179). Her project produced "a model of epistemic justification that is simultaneously naturalized and gynocentric" (Duran, 1991, p. 124).

For all of these feminist empiricists, doing "better science" will eliminate the "bad science" that results from bias (Harding, 1991, p. 111). This improvement requires attention to the knower as much as to the conditions of what is to be known. In other words, the empiricist presupposition of "a uniform, homogeneous 'human nature' that allows any knower to act as a substitute for any other" (Code, 2000, p. 166) is disrupted. Feminist empiricists insist instead that "rigorous empirical investigation of the circumstances of the knowers must be incorporated into scientific and everyday judgments of knowledge [in order] to cleanse the final products of sexism, androcentrism, racism and other specificities" (p. 166).

FEMINIST STANDPOINT EPISTEMOLOGY

A second major type of feminist epistemology is feminist standpoint theory. This "feminist critical theory" (Harding, 2004, p. 1) was developed in the early 1980s by several feminists who were indebted to the historical materialism of Marxism (hence it is sometimes referred to as a "materialist epistemology").[7] Even though they acknowledged that feminist empiricism produced "more adequate knowledge than classical empiricism" (Code, 2000, p. 171), for them it was still not adequate enough. Two of these early standpoint theorists, Nancy Hartsock and Hilary Rose, insisted that a primary weakness resulted from the fact that "empiricists cannot address the historical-material diversity from which people produce knowledge" (Code, 2000, p. 171). In fact, they say, "no version of empiricism—feminist or otherwise—can offer sufficiently radical analyses of the structural factors that shape women's practices and consciousness in 'the everyday world,' where authoritative knowledge derives from the experiences of the dominant" (Code, 2000, p. 461). What was needed, and what standpoint theorists provided, was an analysis of the "relations between the production of knowledge and practices of power" (Harding, 2004, p. 1). Their work "opened a path for feminist research and theory to escape the individualism and voluntarism of the standard empiricist criticisms of researchers' biases that were said to cause sexist and androcentric knowledge claims" (Harding, 2004, p. 18).

To accomplish this, standpoint theorists looked to the Marxist analysis of class and the lives of working people as a model. For example, Nancy Hartsock (2004) argued that "feminist theorizing [must] be grounded in women's material activity" (p. 49). By promoting "a specifically feminist historical materialism," Hartsock felt that we would have "an important epistemological tool for understanding and opposing all forms of domination—a feminist standpoint" (p. 35). She argued that "a standpoint is not simply an interested position (as interpreted as bias) but it is interested in the sense of being engaged" (p. 36). One of the most controversial dimensions of standpoint theory is that this designated, interested standpoint "bestow[s] upon its occupants scientific and epistemic *advantage*" (Harding, 1986, p. 148, emphasis added).

Alison Jaggar (1988) supported the work of standpoint epistemology, especially the notion of epistemic privilege, by elaborating on the advantages of socialist feminism in ending women's oppression. She argued that "the special social or class position of women gives them a special epistemological standpoint which makes possible a view of the world that is more reliable and less distorted than that available either to capitalist or to working-class men" (Jaggar, 2004, p. 56). Furthermore, Jaggar declared that "a primary condition for the adequacy of a feminist theory, indeed for the adequacy of any theory, is that it should represent the world from the standpoint of women" (p. 56).

Clearly, feminist standpoint theory was intended to counter the dominant practices of generalizing all human experience based on the limitations of "white, middle-class, educated men" (Code, 2000, p. 171). By granting de facto epistemic privilege to this limited sector of the population, everyone else, including women, were relegated to "underclass epistemic positions" (p. 171). The critique offered by standpoint theorists underscored "the systematic structural oppression of women, supported by widespread ideologies of women's inferiority" (Harding, 2004, p. 18).

But not only do feminist standpoint theorists criticize the assumed, invisible epistemic privilege of the white male experience, they also criticize other assumptions that permeate traditional philosophy and science. For instance, unlike traditional empirical scientists who dismiss the context of discovery as epistemologically irrelevant, standpoint theorists insist that "the grounds for knowledge are fully saturated with history and social life rather than abstracted from it" (Harding, 2004, p. 128). Standpoint feminists also argue against the view of "universal human problematics" and for the "historicity of specific [knowledge] claims" (pp. 128–129). At the same time, these feminists do not claim to be free of their own background assumptions or specificities; on the contrary, they argue that all knowledge claims "bear the fingerprints of the communities that produce them" (p. 128).

Feminist standpoint theorists have advanced our thinking about the subjects of knowledge, the knower, the inquirer. Their scholarship has provided us with a view considerably different from the traditional empiricist position. For one thing, knowers are "embodied and visible" within a historical context, and this historical embeddedness is not just manifest at the personal or individual level—it is also reflected in "the thought of an age" (Harding, 2004, p. 133). Furthermore, by situating the knower in a particular historical and social location, a "causal symmetry" between the knower and the objects of knowledge is created, since both sides of the epistemological relation have been shaped by similar "social forces" (p. 133). Echoing some of the feminist empiricists we discussed earlier, "communities and not primarily individuals produce knowledge" (p. 133). However, unlike the feminist empiricists, standpoint theorists view "the subjects/agents of knowledge [as] . . . multiple, heterogeneous, and contradictory or incoherent, not unitary, homogeneous, and coherent" (p. 134). This multiplicity and heterogeneity not only derive from differences in individual women's lives, but also mirror "the situation for women as a class. It is the thinker whose consciousness is bifurcated, the outsider within, the marginal person now located at the center . . . who has generated feminist science and new knowledge" (p. 134).

Harding's reference to "the outsider within" derives from the liberatory work of Patricia Hill Collins (1990) and bell hooks (1984). In Collins's own words, we see that "taken together, the outsider-within perspective generated by Black women's location in the labor market and this grounding in traditional African-American culture provide the material backdrop for a unique Black women's standpoint on self and society. As outsiders within, Black women have a distinct view of the contradictions between the dominant group's actions and ideologies" (Collins, 1990, p. 11).

Feminist standpoint theory, like feminist empiricism, provides a critique of the alleged neutrality of mainstream social and natural science. However, going beyond feminist empiricism, standpoint theory shows that "the conceptual frameworks themselves . . . [and] the disciplines [are] complicitous with sexist and androcentric agendas" (Harding, 2004, pp. 4–5). By contesting the "epistemic neutrality" of standard research (Code, 2000, p. 461), the explicitly political "feminist research projects . . . often succeeded in producing empirically more accurate accounts" of the world than purportedly objective methods (Harding, 2004, p. 5). Standpoint feminist research underscored the fact that "androcentric, economically advantaged, racist, Eurocentric, and heterosexist conceptual frameworks ensured systematic ignorance and error about not only the lives of the oppressed, but also about the lives of their oppressors and thus about how nature and social relations in general worked" (p. 5).

Nevertheless, standpoint theorists encountered criticism, from within and beyond their circle. In a self-reflective moment, Alison Jaggar (2004) asked, "If socialist feminist epistemology is accepted, then knowledge must be reconstructed from the standpoint of women. But do all women really occupy the same standpoint? And if they do not, which women occupy the standpoint that is most advantageous?" (p. 63). It is here that even the most radical feminist theory encountered criticism for its "predominately white, middle class origins" (p. 63). As noted earlier, Patricia Hill Collins (1990, 2004) interrupted the taken-for-granted assumptions about "women's experience" that informed feminist standpoint theory. She reminded the predominantly white theorists who were generating this new epistemology and research methodology that not all women have the same standpoint, and hence do not bring the same knowledge and experience to the table. She offered a critique of feminist standpoint theory, particularly the early theory that relied heavily on Marxist theory and epistemology (Tanesini, 1999, p. 152). As an African American woman, Collins (2004) was especially suspicious "of standpoint approaches in Marxist social theory [that] reflect the binary thinking of its Western origins" (p. 270). She goes on to say, "Ironically, by quantifying and ranking human oppressions, standpoint theorists invoke criteria for methodological adequacy that resemble those of positivism" (p. 270). Clearly, Collins would concur that if the point of feminist epistemology is to ensure a more complete, accurate account of the world, then the experiences and standpoint of black women and other women of color and the crucial knowledge they provide must be incorporated into any feminist standpoint theory. But she did not "claim that Black women are more oppressed . . . and therefore have the best standpoint from which to understand the mechanisms, processes, and effects of oppression" (p. 270)—nor, obviously, does this argument from exclusion apply only to black feminists.

Collins's (2004, p. 103) concept of the "outsider within" was a significant contribution to feminist scholarship. In fact, Sandra Harding's later re-visioning of standpoint theory relies greatly on this construct. For Harding, "the perspective of marginal people . . . is a standpoint. . . . Each marginal group has its own perspective, and each of these is partial" (Tanesini, 1999, p. 152). This echoes Collins (2004), who reminds us that "Afro-American women have long been privy to some of the most intimate secrets of white society," which "has provided a special standpoint on self, family and society for Afro-American women" (p. 103). At the same time, she acknowledges that "Black women are not the only outsiders. . . . Black women's experiences highlight the tension experienced by any group of less powerful outsiders encountering the paradigmatic thought of a more powerful insider community. In this sense, a variety of individuals can learn from Black women's experiences as outsiders within: Black men, working-class individuals, white women, other people of color, religious and sexual minorities" (pp. 121–122).

Maria Lugones (1990) is another feminist of color who "emphasizes the need to understand and affirm the plurality in and among women as central to feminist ontology and epistemology" (p. 390). Lugones understands from her own lived experience as a privileged woman from Argentina that we all inhabit different and multiple "worlds." Furthermore, she maintains that as "outsiders to the U.S. mainstream, women of color practice 'world' traveling, mostly out of necessity," and that this experience with different contexts helps form "the acquired flexibility in shifting from the mainstream construction of life to other constructions of life" (p. 390).

How do standpoint feminists argue for a "stronger objectivity" than that obtained through traditional inquiry? Isn't it counterintuitive to think that by being explicitly "political" and "value-laden" you can produce more "objective" knowledge? Sandra Harding (2004) offers an argument for "why it is reasonable to think that the socially situated grounds and subjects of standpoint epistemologies require and generate stronger standards of objectivity than do those that turn away from providing systematic methods for locating knowledge in history" (pp. 127–128). For Harding, "The problem with the conventional conception of objectivity is not that it is too rigorous or too "objectifying," as some have argued, but that it is *not rigorous or objectifying enough;* it is too weak to accomplish even the goals for which it has been designed, let alone the more difficult projects called for by feminisms and other new social movements" (p. 128).

Harding (2004) claims, as do other standpoint theorists, that "'starting off thought' from the lives of marginalized peoples; beginning in those determinate, objective locations . . . will generate illuminating critical questions that do not arise in thought that begins from dominant group lives" and thus will help "generate less partial and distorted accounts not only of women's lives but also of men's lives and of the whole social order" (p. 128). At the same time, Harding concedes that these "epistemologically advantaged starting points for research do not *guarantee* that the researcher can maximize objectivity in her account; these grounds provide only a necessary—not a sufficient starting point for maximizing objectivity" (p. 128, emphasis added).

What does "strong objectivity" mean for Harding and other standpoint theorists? For starters, "strong objectivity requires that the subject of knowledge be placed on the same critical, causal plane as the objects of knowledge" (Harding, 2004, p. 136). Since "beliefs function as evidence at every stage of scientific inquiry," the "individual and the historically located social community . . . must be considered as part of the object of knowledge from the perspective of scientific method" (p. 136). Harding insists that we must become more "self-reflexive" about our "unexamined beliefs" and assumptions as they enter into every stage of the inquiry process including "the selection of problems, the formation of hypotheses, the design of the research (including the organization of research communities), the collection of data, the interpretation and sorting of data, decision about when to stop research, the way results of research are reported, and so on" (p. 136).

Harding (1986) reminds us that both feminist empiricism and feminist standpoint theorists "appear to assert that objectivity never has been and could not be increased by value-neutrality. Instead, it is commitments to antiauthoritarian, antielitist, participatory, and emancipatory values and projects that increase the objectivity of science" (p. 27). Furthermore, she suggests that "standpoint theories not only acknowledge the social situatedness that is the inescapable lot of all knowledge-seeking projects but also, more importantly, transform it into a systematically available scientific resource" (Harding, 2004, p. 129). Harding's notion that "objective knowledge . . . is situated knowledge" resembles that of Donna Haraway (Tanesini, 1999, p. 176). In her now-classic article "Situated Knowledges: The Science Question in Feminism and the Privilege of Partial Perspective," Haraway (1991) argues, "Feminists have to insist on a better account of the world; it is not enough to show radical historical contingency and modes of construction for everything" (p. 187). Referring to Harding's notion of "successor science projects," Haraway maintains that "feminists have stakes in a successor science project that offers a more adequate, richer, better account of a world, in order to live in it well and in critical, reflexive relation to our own as well as others' practices of domination and the unequal part of privilege and oppression that make up all positions" (p. 187). Haraway describes what she sees as an ethical and political problem, as much as an

epistemological one: "how to have *simultaneously* an account of radical historical contingency for all knowledge claims and knowing subjects, a critical
practice for recognizing our own 'semiotic technologies' for making meanings, *and* a no-nonsense commitment to faithful accounts of a 'real' world"
(p. 187).

Like Harding, Haraway (1991) acknowledges the "contradictory and
necessary" dimension of the "need for a successor science project and a postmodern insistence on irreducible difference and radical multiplicity of local knowledges" (p. 187). She argues against the kind of "objectivity that
promises transcendence, a story that loses track of its mediations just where
someone might be held responsible for something, and unlimited instru-
mental power" (p. 187). In her inimitable manner, Haraway acknowledges
the challenge she is posing:

> In our efforts to climb the greased pole leading to a usable doctrine
> of objectivity, I and most other feminists in the objectivity debates
> have alternatively, or even simultaneously, held on to both ends
> of the dichotomy, which Harding describes in terms of successor
> science projects versus postmodernist accounts of difference and I
> have sketched . . . as radical constructivism versus feminist critical
> empiricism. It is, of course, hard to climb when you are holding on
> to both ends of a pole, simultaneously or alternately. It is, therefore,
> time to switch metaphors. (p. 188)

The metaphor Haraway seeks is "vision" to address the problem of "binary oppositions" and dualisms (p. 188). To this end Haraway develops "a
doctrine of embodied objectivity that accommodates paradoxical and critical feminist science projects" (p. 188). For her, "feminist objectivity means
quite simply *situated knowledges*" (p. 188).

By "insisting metaphorically on the particularity and embodiment of all
vision . . . and not giving in to the tempting myths of vision as a route to
disembodiment," Haraway (1991) argues that this "allows us to construct
a usable, but not an innocent, doctrine of objectivity" (p. 189). This version of "objectivity turns out to be about particular and specific embodiment, and definitely not about the false vision promising transcendence of
all limits and responsibility" (p. 190). For her, "the moral is simple: only
partial perspective promises objective vision" (p. 190). She goes on to say
that "feminist objectivity is about limited location and situated knowledge,

not about transcendence and splitting of subject and object. In this way we might become answerable for what we learn how to see" (p. 190). It is this accountability and responsibility for how and what we construct as knowledge that is paramount for Haraway.[8]

What makes Haraway (1991) particularly compelling in the feminist context is that, although she advocates for "situated and embodied knowledges and against various forms of unlocatable, and so irresponsible, knowledge claims" (p. 191), she also grasps the "danger of romanticizing and/or appropriating the vision of the less powerful" (p. 191). Haraway offers a cautionary caveat of standpoint theory: "the standpoints of the subjugated are not 'innocent' positions" and "to see from below is neither easily learned nor unproblematic" (p. 191). At the same time, she thinks "they are preferred because in principle they are least likely to allow denial of the critical and interpretive core of all knowledge" (p. 191). Because "the subjugated have a decent chance to be on to the god-trick . . . [they] are preferred because they seem to promise more adequate, sustained, objective, transforming accounts of the world" (p. 191).

Haraway's theory "constitutes a real break with the dominant account of knowledge in terms of representations" (Tanesini, 1999, p. 180). She attacks relativism and totalization, for they "are both 'god-tricks' promising vision from everywhere and nowhere, equally and fully, common myths in rhetorics surrounding Science" (Haraway, 1991, p. 191). Rather, "*it is precisely in the politics and epistemology of partial perspectives that the possibility of sustained, rational, objective enquiry rests*" (p. 191, emphasis added). At the same time, she cautions us that "not just any partial perspective will do; we must be hostile to easy relativisms and holisms built out of summing and subsuming parts" (p. 192). She argues for "a doctrine and practice of objectivity that privileges contestation, deconstruction, passionate construction, webbed connections, and hope for transformation of systems of knowledges and ways of seeing" (pp. 191–192). Borrowing from Annette Kuhn (1982), Haraway promotes a "'passionate detachment' [that] requires more than acknowledged and self-critical partiality. We are also bound to seek perspective from those points of view, which can never be known in advance, which promise something quite extraordinary, that is, knowledge potent for constructing worlds less organized by axes of domination" (p. 192).

Haraway (1991) invokes Harding's notion of a "successor science" that is accompanied by "postmodern sensibilities" (p. 192). She says that "the ground for any believable claim to objectivity or rationality not riddled with

. . . denials and repressions" combines "the hope for transformative knowl-edge" with "the severe check and stimulus of sustained critical enquiry" (p. 192). This "feminist doctrine of rationality and objectivity," like much of science, is both "utopian and visionary" (p. 192).

Haraway (1991) claims that "the promise of objectivity" entails "a sci-entific knower [who] seeks the subject position not of identity, but of ob-jectivity; that is, partial connection" (p. 193). She elaborates by saying that "there is no way to 'be' simultaneously in all, or wholly in any, of the privi-leged (subjugated) positions structured by gender, race, nation, and class. The search for such a 'full' and total position is the search for the fetishized perfect subject of oppositional history, sometimes appearing in feminist theory as the essentialized Third World Woman" (p. 193). Haraway's "com-mitment to mobile positioning and to passionate detachment is dependent on the impossibility of innocent 'identity' politics and epistemologies as strategies for seeing from the standpoints of the subjugated in order to see well" (p. 192).

Haraway also doubts whether the position of the knower can ever be a unitary self; instead she prefers to think that "the split and contradictory self is the one who can interrogate positionings and be accountable, the one who can construct and join rational conversations and fantastic imaginings that change history. Splitting, not being, is the privileged image for feminist epistemologies of scientific knowledge. . . . The knowing self is partial in all its guises, never finished, whole, simply there and original; it is always constructed and stitched together without claiming to be another" (p. 193).

This move toward multiple subjectivities and multiple positionings, and resistance to essentializing/ed identities begins to anticipate what Hard-ing refers to as "postmodernist accounts of difference" (Haraway, 1991, p. 188), and offers a segue into the last section of this chapter, where our focus turns to the contributions that postmodernism and poststructuralism have made to feminist theory, epistemology, and inquiry.

FEMINIST POSTMODERNISM AND POSTSTRUCTURALISM

A third framework for feminist theory and philosophy is informed by the influences of postmodernist and poststructuralist thought. Nancy Fraser and Linda Nicholson (1990) describe the relation between postmodernism and feminism as one of "mutual wariness"; yet they maintain that "there are good reasons for exploring the relations between [the two]" (p. 19). Indeed, we see several points in common between postmodernism and feminism, especially their attempts "to develop new paradigms of social criticism" and "to rethink the relation between philosophy and social criticism" (p. 19).

In exploring "the prospect of a postmodern feminism" (p. 20), Fraser and Nicholson pursued these questions: How can we combine a postmodernist incredulity toward metanarratives with the social-critical power of feminism? How can we conceive a version of criticism without philosophy which is robust enough to handle the tough job of analyzing sexism in all its endless variety and monotonous similarity? (p. 34). They answer these questions by proposing some characteristics of a postmodern-feminist theory. To begin with, this theoretical perspective "would be nonuniversalist . . . and would replace unitary notions of woman and feminine gender identity with plural and complexly constructed conceptions of social identity" (pp. 34–35). It "would be pragmatic and fallibilistic . . . tailor[ing] its methods and categories to the specific task at hand, using multiple categories when appropriate for forswearing the metaphysical comfort of a single feminist method or feminist epistemology" (p. 35). And, they argue, such a theory would be very useful "for contemporary feminist political practice . . . practice [that] is increasingly a matter of alliances rather than one of unity around a universally shared interest or identity" (p. 35). The valorization of multiple over unitary identities and subjectivities, and the focus on difference, bridges postmodern feminism with standpoint feminism more than with cultural or radical feminism, which still adhere to "dichotomies and absolutes connected with . . . an essential nature of womanhood" (Weiner, 1995, p. 63).

The antiessentialist, antifoundationalist stance prevalent in postmodern theory is particularly strong in some varieties of poststructuralist thought that have been taken up by feminists. Chris Weedon (1987), one of the first feminist scholars to craft a specific position on poststructuralist theory that is compatible with feminism, reminds us of the theoretical differences that make a difference. For her, "not all forms [of poststructuralism] are necessarily productive for feminism" (p. 20). Weedon and others recognize the importance for feminism of the poststructuralist emphasis on "meaning, subjectivity and power" (Code, 2000, p. 397). Yet, just as "feminist" signifies multiple meanings, "the term 'poststructuralist' . . . like all language, [is] plural. It does not have one fixed meaning but is generally applied to a range of theoretical positions" (Weedon, 1987, p. 19). Indeed, the impossibility of securing one "essential meaning" of a word or concept itself reflects one of the key elements of a poststructuralist outlook.

Poststructuralism and feminism have some of the same similarities that Fraser and Nicholson (1990) identified between postmodernism and feminism. As with certain dominant strands of feminism, Peters and Burbules (2004) point out that "poststructuralism at its broadest level offers a philosophical attack upon the scientific pretensions of social inquiry, including a critique of Enlightenment norms that educational research typically prides itself on: 'truth,' 'objectivity' and 'progress'" (p. 4). Just as feminist philosophy has been committed to a critique of the way knowledge is produced and validated, so too "poststructuralism aims to expose structures of domination by diagnosing 'power/knowledge' relations and their manifestations in our classifications, examinations, practices, and institutions" (p. 5).

Weedon (1987) maintains, "Feminist interests have placed subjectivity, signifying practices, and sexuality on the theoretical agenda and focused attention on the political implications of many of the theories which have formed current poststructuralist perspectives" (p. 12). As two different critical theories, feminism and poststructuralism each deconstruct the taken-for-granted, received knowledge, "call[ing] into question the naturalness of the disciplines, stressing that disciplines are historical formations" (Peters & Burbules, 2004, p. 5). Furthermore, similar to some strands of feminist epistemology, "poststructuralism . . . adopts an anti- or post-epistemological standpoint and is fiercely anti-foundationalist. It also adopts an anti-realist position, . . . rejecting the established picture of knowledge as an accurate representation" (p. 4).

As Lorraine Code (2000) reminds us, "Poststructuralist and postmodern feminists argue, following Foucault, that knowledge and power are integrally related and that knowledge is partial—both incomplete and representing particular interests" (p. 398). Further, relying on nonfoundationalist epistemologies, poststructuralist feminists insist that "knowledge should be judged not by reference to truth claims but by its effects in the world" (p. 399).

Not everyone, however, is comfortable with the expression "feminist poststructuralism" or "poststructuralist feminism." Elizabeth St. Pierre and Wanda Pillow (2000), for example, argue that these terms are "insufficient for describing the complex[ity]" of the theoretical intersections between the two (p. 3). They prefer the conjunction and to show "how the two theories/movements work similarly and differently to trouble foundational ontologies, methodologies, and epistemologies" (p. 2). Their deployment of "feminist *and* poststructural [points to] a relation that gestures toward fluid and multiple dislocations and alliances" (p. 3)—and in which the theoretical influences flow in both directions (see also St. Pierre, 2000).

Peters and Burbules (2004) also raise concerns about the idea of feminist poststructuralism. In particular, they object to the attempt to "homogenize the 'French poststructuralist feminist'" because "the women writers [in this category] are very different from one another . . . it is difficult to characterize a 'movement' here in any strict sense" (p. 73). For example, although poststructuralist thought interrogates "the status of the rational subject of western thought," and has replaced "rational, intentional subjectivity" with other notions (Code, 2000, p. 398), it is done differently by different theorists. With Lacan, for instance, "subjectivity is split"; with Kristeva, Irigaray, and Foucault it is "discursively produced"; with Kristeva it is "in process"; and with Lacan, Irigaray, and Kristeva, it is "the effect of unconscious as well as conscious forces" (p. 398). At the same time, when "taken together, their work does represent an important aspect of French poststructuralism—some would argue cutting edge" (Peters & Burbules, 2004, p. 73).

For this volume, however, while acknowledging the aforementioned caveats, we employ the term *feminist poststructuralism* to articulate a particular strand of feminist theory that has had a substantial impact on educational research—including the work of people like St. Pierre and Pillow who eschew the label. We accept, provisionally, Weedon's (1987) effort to offer a concise and coherent look at the different connections feminists have made to poststructuralist theory to study "gendered subjectivity" (p. 43). She insists, "Feminism has taken the dual paths of appropriating existing theories to its needs and of attempting to develop radical alternative theories" (p. 18). In her construction of feminist poststructuralism, Weedon includes psychoanalytic understandings and explanations (p. 87) as well as theories of "discourse, power, and resistance" (p. 107). With regard to the latter, Weedon shows "how poststructural theory can produce politically useful understanding of the production and reproduction of patriarchal forms of power, both institutionally and for individual women and men" (p. 107).

The work of Michel Foucault, for example, has been appropriated in significant ways by many feminist education researchers who see the usefulness of Foucauldian discourse analysis. In a later chapter we explore some of these feminist educational researchers in more detail. But as a preliminary introduction, we find the work of Elizabeth St. Pierre and Wanda Pillow (2000) and their colleagues in *Working the Ruins: Feminist Poststructural*

Theory and Methods in Education very useful. St. Pierre and Pillow introduce their edited volume on feminist poststructuralism with reference to what Linda Nicholson has called the "twilight of foundationalism" (St. Pierre & Pillow, 2000, p. 1; see Nicholson, 1999, p. 117). Nicholson, as well as St. Pierre and Pillow, points to a time "after the crises of representation and legitimation, and through and out of a restless 'post' period that troubles all those things we assumed were solid, substantial, and whole—knowledge, truth, reality, reason, science, progress, the subject and so forth" (St. Pierre & Pillow, 2000, p. 1). The authors embrace the phrase "to trouble" in association with poststructuralism. They see that "poststructuralism in all its manifestations, along with other 'posts' that describe continuing skepticism about regimes of truth that have failed us, has worked the ruins of humanism's version of those concepts" (p. 1). "Troubling" is their version of a postmodern "incredulity toward metanarratives" and describes their effort to "ask questions that produce different knowledge and produce knowledge differently" (p. 1). Like many poststructural authors (Derrida, Spivak, and others), they want to both invoke and appeal to concepts and values while bracketing them as potentially problematic and worthy of critical reassessment; "troubling" concepts is a way of both referring to them and questioning them.

St. Pierre and Pillow (2000) also build on the work of feminist poststructuralists and deconstructionists such as Trinh Min Ha, who practice a "radical openness" that gives rise to "different structures of intelligibility that, in turn, produce different epistemologies, ontologies, and methodologies" (p. 2). St. Pierre and Pillow resist the critique of some feminists who think that poststructuralist theory is bad for feminism, that it is apolitical, or even that it is fundamentally conservative (p. 1). Instead, they insist that "feminists and poststructuralists have worked together and separately . . . to facilitate structural failures in some of foundationalism's most heinous formations—racism, patriarchy, homophobia, ageism, and so forth—the ruins out of which they now work" (p. 2). Included in this effort are scholars in their collection whose "work moves toward a reconfigured social science" (p. 3). They cite Patti Lather, their teacher and colleague, who argues for a "'less comfortable social science' . . . (one that tries to be 'accountable to complexity')" (pp. 3–4). This commitment to accountability resembles in some ways that of feminist empirical and standpoint theorists; however, Lather and her colleagues want to disrupt or trouble the notion of accountability at the same time. They are less interested than other feminist colleagues in seeking more accurate accounts of the world than traditional social inquiry.

When they trouble the waters, or "work the ruins," these authors are taking a cue from Derrida as "the work toward the not-yet-thought" (St. Pierre & Pillow, 2000, p. 4). They are producing "postfoundational theoretical and political positions, including feminist, race, critical, queer and postcolonial theories" that subvert what they see as the exclusionary themes of humanism (p. 5). It is with this feminist challenge to mainstream social science research in hand that we can now turn to explore the complexities and contradictions, as well as contributions to social inquiry, of feminist research methodologies.

NOTES

1. See, for example, Alison M. Jaggar (1988), *Feminist Politics and Human Nature*.
2. See, for example, the edited collection by Ann Garry and Marilyn Pearsall (1989), *Women, Knowledge and Reality: Explorations in Feminist Philosophy*.
3. It is important to remember that the feminist critique of philosophy in general, and of epistemology in particular, did not occur in a vacuum. The dominant positivist conceptions of knowledge and knowing had been challenged in earlier decades by Kuhn and Quine (Harding, 2004, p. xiii), opening the way for criticisms of science, the philosophy of science, and the theory of knowledge that informed them.
4. In doing so, we also want to offer one caveat: we recognize the danger in making generalizations about epistemology as if it were a unitary concept—when in fact there are divergences within disciplinary subfields.
5. Definition from the 1967 *Encyclopedia of Philosophy* as quoted in Harding (1991, pp. 106–107).
6. Patti Lather, a leading feminist theorist and methodologist, after engaging in post, and "post-post" discourses, has become less interested in "better" science, wanting to move beyond this notion. See Lather (2007) for her freshest account of this position.
7. For example, see the work of Nancy Hartsock (1983), Dorothy Smith (1987), and Hilary Rose (1983).
8. We will return to this theme of "noninnocence," accountability, and responsibility when we address Patti Lather's (2007) most recent work.

REFERENCES

Alcoff, L. (Ed.). (1998). *Epistemology: The big questions*. Malden, MA: Blackwell.
Alcoff, L., & Potter, E. (Eds.). (1993). *Feminist epistemologies*. New York: Routledge.

Antony, L. (1993). Quine as feminist: The radical import of naturalized epistemology. In L. Antony & C. Witt (Eds.), *A mind of one's own: Feminist essays on reason and objectivity* (pp. 185–225). Boulder, CO: Westview.

Code, L. (1998). Epistemology. In A. Jaggar & I.M. Young (Eds.), *A companion to feminist philosophy* (pp. 175–184). Malden, MA: Blackwell.

Code, L. (Ed.). (2000). *Encyclopedia of feminist theories.* London: Routledge.

Cole, E.B. (1993). *Philosophy and feminist criticism: An introduction.* New York: Paragon House.

Collins, P.H. (1990). *Black feminist thought: Knowledge, consciousness and the politics of empowerment.* Boston: Unwin Hyman.

Collins, P.H. (2004). Learning from the outsider within: The sociological significance of black feminist thought. In S. Harding (Ed.), *The feminist standpoint theory reader: Intellectual and political controversies* (pp. 103–126). New York: Routledge.

Duran, J. (1991). *Toward a feminist epistemology.* Lanham, MD: Rowman and Littlefield.

Fraser, N., & Nicholson, L. (1990). Social criticism without philosophy: An encounter between feminism and postmodernism. In L. Nicholson (Ed.), *Feminism/postmodernism* (pp. 19–38). New York: Routledge.

Garry, A., & Pearsall, M. (Eds.). (1989). *Women, knowledge and reality: Explorations in feminist philosophy.* Boston: Unwin Hyman.

Gatens, M. (1998). Modern Rationalism. In A. Jaggar & I.M. Young (Eds.), *A companion to feminist philosophy* (pp. 21–29). Malden, MA: Blackwell.

Haraway, D. (1991). *Simians, cyborgs and women: The reinvention of nature.* New York: Routledge.

Harding, S. (1986). *The science question in feminism.* Ithaca, NY: Cornell University Press.

Harding, S. (1991). *Whose science? Whose knowledge? Thinking from women's lives.* Milton Keynes, UK: Open University Press.

Harding, S. (1993). Rethinking standpoint epistemology: What is "strong objectivity"? In L. Alcoff & E. Potter (Eds.), *Feminist epistemologies* (pp. 49–82). New York: Routledge.

Harding, S. (Ed.). (2004). *The feminist standpoint theory reader: Intellectual and political controversies.* New York: Routledge.

Harding, S., & Hintikka, M. (Eds.). (1983). *Discovering reality: Feminist perspectives on epistemology, metaphysics, methodology, and philosophy of science.* Dordrecht, Holland: D. Reidel.

Hartsock, N. (1983). *Money, sex, and power: Toward a feminist historical materialism.* Boston: Northeastern University Press.

Hartsock, N. (1998). *The feminist standpoint revisited and other essays.* Boulder, CO: Westview.

Hartsock, N. (2004). The feminist standpoint: Developing the ground for a specifically feminist historical materialism. In S. Harding (Ed.), *The feminist standpoint theory reader: Intellectual and political controversies* (pp. 35–53). New York: Routledge.

hooks, b. (1984). *Feminist theory: From margin to center.* Boston: South End Press.

Jaggar, A. (1988). *Feminist politics and human nature.* Lanham, MD: Rowman and Littlefield.

Jaggar, A. (2004). Feminist politics and epistemology: The standpoint of women. In S. Harding (Ed.), *The feminist standpoint theory reader: Intellectual and political controversies* (pp. 55–66). New York: Routledge.

Kim, J. (1998). What is "naturalized epistemology"? In L. Alcoff (Ed.), *Epistemology: The big questions* (pp. 265–284). Malden, MA: Blackwell.

Kuhn, A. (1982). Passionate detachment. In *Women's pictures: Feminism and cinema.* London: Verso.

Lather, P. (1991). *Getting smart: Feminist research and pedagogy with/in the postmodern.* New York: Routledge.

Lather, P. (2007). *Getting lost: Feminist efforts toward a double(d) science.* Albany: State University of New York Press.

Lloyd, G. (1993). *The man of reason: "Male" and "female" in Western philosophy.* Minneapolis: University of Minnesota Press.

Longino, H. (1990). *Science as social knowledge: Values and objectivity in scientific inquiry.* Princeton, NJ: Princeton University Press.

Longino, H. (1993a). Essential tensions—phase two: Feminist, philosophical, and social studies of science. In L. Antony & C. Witt (Eds.), *A mind of one's own: Feminist essays on reason and objectivity* (pp. 257–272). Boulder, CO: Westview.

Longino, H. (1993b). Subjects, power and knowledge: Description and prescription in feminist philosophies of science. In L. Alcoff & E. Potter (Eds.), *Feminist epistemologies* (pp. 101–120). New York: Routledge.

Lugones, M. (1990). Playfulness, "world"-traveling and loving perception. In G. Anzaldua (Ed.), *Making face, making soul* (pp. 390–402). San Francisco: Aunt Lute.

Nelson, L.H. (1990). *Who knows: From Quine to a feminist empiricism.* Philadelphia: Temple University Press.

Nelson, L.H. (1993). Epistemological communities. In L. Alcoff & E. Potter (Eds.), *Feminist epistemologies* (pp. 121–159). New York: Routledge.

Nelson, L.H. (1998). Empiricism. In A. Jaggar & I.M. Young (Eds.), *A companion to feminist philosophy* (pp. 30–38). Malden, MA: Blackwell.

Nelson, L.H. (1999). The very idea of feminist epistemology. In E. Bianchi (Ed.), *Is feminist philosophy philosophy?* (pp. 167–189). Chicago: Northwestern University Press.

Nicholson, L. (Ed.). (1990). *Feminism/postmodernism.* New York: Routledge.

Nicholson, L. (1999). *The play of reason: From the modern to the postmodern.* Ithaca, NY: Cornell University Press.

Peters, M., & Burbules, N. (2004). *Poststructuralism and educational research.* Lanham, MD: Rowman and Littlefield.

Phillips, D.C., & Burbules, N. (2000). *Postpositivism and educational research.* Lanham, MD: Rowman and Littlefield.

Quine, W.V.O. (1998). Epistemology naturalized. In L. Alcoff (Ed.), *Epistemology: The big questions* (pp. 253–265). Malden, MA: Blackwell.

Rose, H. (1983). Hand, brain and heart: A feminist epistemology for the natural sciences. *Signs,* 9(11), 73–90.

Smith, D. (1987). *The everyday world as problematic: A feminist sociology.* Boston: Northeastern University Press.

St. Pierre, E. (2000). Poststructural feminism in education: An overview. *Qualitative Studies in Education,* 13(5), 477–515.

St. Pierre, E., & Pillow, W. (Eds.). (2000). *Working the ruins: Feminist poststructural theory and methods in education.* New York: Routledge.

Tanesini, A. (1999). *An introduction to feminist epistemologies.* Malden, MA: Blackwell.

Tuana, N., & Tong, R. (Eds.). (1995). *Feminism and philosophy: Essential readings in theory, reinterpretation, and application.* Boulder, CO: Westview.

Weedon, C. (1987). *Feminist practice and poststructuralist theory.* Oxford, UK: Basil Blackwell.

Weiner, G. (1995). *Feminisms in education: An introduction.* Buckingham: Open University Press.

CHAPTER 4

Feminist Inquiry

INTRODUCTION

With this historicized mapping of feminism and a review of some of the significant philosophical concerns raised by feminist theory, we can now proceed to a discussion of what it means to conduct "feminist-based inquiry" (Nielsen, 1990, p. 1) and whether there is "a distinctive feminist method of inquiry" (Harding, 1987b, p. 1). Just as it is not easy to define or categorize feminism, we also recognize here the complexity in answering the query, "What is feminist methodology?" (DeVault, 1999, p. 21). By recollecting the feminist epistemological frameworks that have already been discussed, this chapter examines several different perspectives on feminist inquiry. We also explore the contested terrain of feminist research through the debates over such questions as: What is the role of a feminist researcher? What kinds of questions does a feminist researcher ask? Is there a distinctive focus for feminist research? What ethical, social, or political commitments accompany this type of research? And we offer examples of wider research approaches and methodologies that have shaped feminist educational research (see also Symposium, 2008).

Of course, none of these topics will have singular or uncontested answers. Given the plurality of feminisms and the many feminist challenges to traditional scientific and social scientific inquiry, there will be, necessarily, a plurality of approaches to feminist research: approaches dependent on the varied assumptions brought to the endeavor by different feminist researchers. It is our hope that by exploring the connections between the epistemological, ethical, and political assumptions held by diverse feminists, we can offer some insight into the range of feminist research being done and the contradictions and challenges faced by these researchers, while still highlighting some broad common themes and concerns.

Over the past three decades of active feminist research, many scholars, including an influential number from education, have weighed in on these issues (see Fonow & Cook, 1991, 2005; Roberts, 1981; Reinharz, 1992; Harding, 1987a, 2004; Stanley, 1990; Stanley & Wise, 1983, 1993; DeVault, 1999; Nielsen, 1990; Lather, 1991, 2007; Bloom, 1998; Fine, 1992; Britzman, 2000, 2003; Olesen, 1994, 2000, 2005). Paralleling the development of feminism and feminist theory, the literature on feminist research methodology reflects the sociocultural and historical context in which it is situated. Similar to our task in chapter 2, when representing the transformational development of feminism and feminist thought, we are presented here with the challenge of how to define uniquely feminist methodologies and methods.

As Virginia Olesen (2005, p. 238) indicates, "complexity and controversy characterize the qualitative feminist research enterprise." Feminists continue to grapple with "the nature of research, the definition of and relationship with those with whom research is done, the characteristics and location of the researcher, and the creation and presentation of knowledges" (p. 238). Olesen sums up her query when she says: "If there is a dominant theme [in feminist research], it is the question of knowledges. Whose knowledges? Where and how obtained, and by whom; from whom and for what purposes?" (p. 238). These questions serve as a framework for the following discussion of feminist methodology and inquiry.

So much of contemporary social and philosophical research takes for granted the early contributions of feminists from the 1960s and 1970s—contributions that were groundbreaking and even revolutionary at the time. Situating feminist research historically is a useful reminder to see just how far we have come. Also, analyzing feminist research in the context of other critical challenges to the received understanding of scientific inquiry will help clarify the distinctive contributions offered by feminism as well as its relations with other intellectual and political trends. In the next section we review what traditional (social) science means by "method" and the various challenges to it. This will put into relief the reasons why feminist scholars felt a need to develop alternative approaches to inquiry, and how their approaches are similar to and different from other oppositional modes of inquiry, such as the hermeneutical and critical theory traditions (see, for example, the work of Brian Fay, 1987, 1996; Richard Bernstein, 1976, 1983; Joyce Nielsen, 1990; and Marsha Westkott, 1990).

THE RECEIVED UNDERSTANDING OF SCIENTIFIC METHOD AND ITS CHALLENGES

In an earlier chapter, we analyzed the mainstream epistemological positions on knowledge, knowing, and the knower. In this section, we outline how these epistemological traditions underlie mainstream approaches to scientific and social scientific inquiry, including educational research. Our previous discussion of epistemologies noted the dominance of rationalism and empiricism in Western philosophical discourse. In the modern scientific context, these two positions, with their foundationalist epistemologies, still shape understandings of the scientific method. In fact, as noted in our introduction, there has been a resurgence of state-sponsored empiricism through the demand for scientific evidence-based research, particularly in the context of educational research, policy, and practice

As Joyce Nielsen (1990, pp. 4–5) indicates: "We can tentatively and briefly define scientific method as including an appeal to empirical evidence, experimentation (defined as the purposeful manipulation of physical matter or events in order to gauge their effects), and the use of inductive and deductive logic." The scientific method, as it is commonly understood, rests on several interrelated assumptions that have particular implications for feminist inquiry. We refer here to the view "that the social world is knowable . . . in the same way that the natural world is knowable—that is, through observation and recording of what appears as 'objective' reality by a subjective (independent) researcher." Furthermore, this "subjective knower should not infect objective truth—that evaluative concerns of the subjective knower should be excluded." This "knowledge-generating approach . . . emphasizes rationality . . . , impersonality . . . , and prediction and control" (pp. 4–5). These assumptions about "objectivity" are inextricably linked to what Richard Bernstein (1983, p. 7) has called "the central cultural opposition of our time": the dichotomy between objectivism and relativism.

Bernstein (1983) defines objectivism as: "the basic conviction that there is or must be some permanent, ahistorical matrix or framework to which we can ultimately appeal in determining the nature of rationality, knowledge, truth, reality, goodness, or rightness." This contrasts for Bernstein with "relativism . . . the basic conviction that when we turn to the examination of those concepts that philosophers have taken to be the most fundamental . . . we are forced to recognize that in the final analysis all such concepts must be understood as relative to a specific conceptual scheme, theoretical framework, paradigm, form of life, society, or culture." Elaborating further, Bernstein says that "objectivism has been closely linked with an acceptance of a basic metaphysical or epistemological distinction between the subject and the object. What is 'out there' (objective) is presumed to be independent of us (subjects), and knowledge is achieved when a subject correctly mirrors or represents objective reality" (pp. 8–9).

As we indicated in our review of epistemological history, modern relativists maintain "that all knowledge is culture-bound, theory-bound, and/or historically specific—that is understandable and valid only within a specific time, place, theory, or perspective" (Nielsen, 1990, p. 3). This is contrary to the assumption of modern science, favoring "generalizations that hold true across time and place and in many different conditions or situations" (p. 5). Feminists find this tension between objectivity and subjectivity, as well as that between objectivity and relativity, central to their work in developing a distinctly feminist approach to inquiry.

The latter half of the twentieth century provided "a virtual revolution in our understanding of the 'image of science'—at least when compared with the so-called orthodox understanding of science advocated by positivists and logical empiricists" (Bernstein, 1976, p. xvi). Bernstein and others agree that we are now in a "postempirical period" with regard to scientific and social scientific inquiry. Several important philosophical and scientific developments have transformed our taken-for-granted, received understanding of science and the scientific method. By the 1970s, the empirical scientific method was no longer considered the only or "ultimate test of knowledge or basis for claims to truth" (Nielsen, 1990, p. 7). On the one hand, we had the nonfoundationalist "critical rationalism" of Karl Popper (Bernstein, 1983, p. 4) competing with the provocative work of Paul Feyerabend (1975), *Against Method,* which "ridicule[d] the belief that there is a determinate scientific method that guides the way in which science and living scientists really work" (Bernstein, 1983, p. xi). And of course Thomas

Kuhn (1962), who "demythologized" science and challenged its infallibility with his work *The Structure of Scientific Revolutions* (Nielsen, 1990, p. 12), "gave expression to and helped identify issues that were erupting from a wide variety of sources" (Bernstein, 1983, p. 21).

Although Kuhn's theory has been questioned, it has been widely influential in changing the way science is understood. Post-Kuhnians now accept science "as a social-historical process of paradigm transitions" instead of "a cumulative process of the discovery of increasingly correct descriptions of the physical world" (Nielsen, 1990, p. 12). Furthermore, they view "science as an activity" and the "content of scientific understanding [as including] not only theories and laws but also metaphysical commitments, exemplars, puzzles, anomalies" and so on (Addelson, 1991, p. 17). Paradigms are theory-laden and culture-laden (Nielsen, 1990, p. 13), which situates their truth claims in specific social, historical, and institutional dynamics. The rise of social studies of science as a research program has documented the ways in which scientific practices actually work to negotiate and socially adjudicate knowledge claims.

Another influence, of course, that has contributed to this postempirical era is post-Newtonian physics, which transformed our thinking about physical reality. Quantum physics encouraged "holistic, ecological, systemic" explanations, rendering obsolete "an older, more mechanistic worldview that underlies the assumptions of both Newtonian physics and traditional scientific methods" (Nielsen, 1990, p. 15).

Parallel to these changes in scientific thinking have been developments in the philosophy of social sciences and as well as in critical and hermeneutical theory. The 1970s were energized by a robust philosophical and political debate between two giants: Hans-Georg Gadamer and Jürgen Habermas. Gadamer's *Truth and Method* (1975) and Habermas's *Knowledge and Human Interests* (1971) offered a platform for exploring the differences between explanations and understandings; and between critical, empirico-analytic, and hermeneutical ways of knowing. Gadamer critiqued the "basic [Cartesian] dichotomy between the subjective and the objective; the conception of knowledge as being a correct representation of what is objective; the conviction that human reason can completely free itself of bias, prejudice, and tradition; the ideal of a universal method by which we can first secure firm foundations of knowledge and then build the edifice of a universal science; the belief that by the power of self-reflection we can transcend our historical context and horizon and know things as they really are in themselves" (Bernstein, 1983, p. 36). Researchers drawing on this hermeneutic tradition "are concerned with the importance of meaning in social interaction and argue that limiting research to observable human action misses the most important part of the story. To explain and understand any human behavior, they argue, we need to know the meaning attached to it by the participants themselves" (Nielsen, 1990, p. 7).

Meanwhile, the critical theory of Jürgen Habermas offered "a critical reexamination of the social and political disciplines and the legacy of positivism in the twentieth century" (Bernstein, 1983, pp. 42–43). Although Habermas recognized the power of Gadamer's philosophical hermeneutics, he felt it "lacked an explicit critical function." Through his ideology-critique, Habermas examined the instrumentalist tendency of modern scientific knowledge to serve, all too often, those in power. In his work, he "argued for the necessity of a dialectical synthesis of empirical-analytic science and hermeneutics into a critical theory [which] has a practical intent and is governed by an emancipatory cognitive interest" (Bernstein, 1983, pp. 42–43). This practical, critical rationality, with criteria for assessing the relative value of social practices and institutions, was an essential dimension of Habermas's critical theory.

Brian Fay (1987) incorporated the Frankfurt School critique of science and knowledge into his account of a critical social science. For Fay, "critical social science is an attempt to understand in a rationally responsible manner the oppressive features of a society such that this understanding stimulates its audience to transform their society and thereby liberate themselves." Resonating with the oft-cited quote from Marx's *Theses on Feuerbach*: "Heretofore the philosophers have only *interpreted* the world, in various ways; the point, however, is to *change* it," Fay's work is committed to "developing, exploring, and criticizing a certain model of social science." For Fay and other critical theorists, it is not a matter of whether social science should be "scientific" or not, but what that means; he argues that "it is possible for critical social science to be fully scientific" and in fact, he "insist[s] on its scientific character." However, for Fay, it is important that critical social science "be at once *scientific, critical* and *practical*" (pp. 4, 5, 7).

For critical theory, it is part of the test of the theoretical adequacy of social science to understand and assess its practical impact on the world it studies; it is an essential aspect of social inquiry that it partly constitutes and shapes the reality it seeks to describe—not as a separate aspect or stage of inquiry, but as integral to the social processes of research and publication itself. Unlike other areas of scientific inquiry, the subjects of social inquiry can read and be influenced by what is said and written about them. This introduces the likelihood of self-fulfilling prophecies and other feedback effects in both the doing and dissemination of social research, and imposes on social researchers a unique set of moral and political responsibilities to reflect upon such effects in the conception and execution of their studies.

Feminist theory and research found an ally in this tradition of critical theory. From the start, as we saw in earlier chapters, feminism is first and foremost a political movement interested in changing the conditions of women for the better. It never pretended to be neutral or objective, removed from the lived reality of real women. It did not rely on abstract, ahistorical, decontextualized understandings of women's experience. Nor did it shy away from having a value-oriented intention to transform society. Like the critical theory of Habermas, feminist theory had an emancipatory purpose, with a strong commitment to connect theory with practice and action. Furthermore, as we have seen, many feminists and critical theorists "argue that there is no such thing as an objectively neutral or disinterested perspective, that everyone or every group (including themselves) is located socially and historically, and that this context inevitably influences the knowledge they produce. Knowledge, in short, is socially constructed" (Nielsen, 1990, p. 9). Finally, the emphasis of critical theory, in Fay's formulation, to give people the resources and understandings that will enable them to liberate themselves fits closely with feminism's orientation toward women's empowerment.

Brian Fay (1987) further maintains that "critical theories and the politics they have inspired are important ingredients of modern life. Most notably, Marxism, feminism and some forms of politicized Freudianism have moved millions of people in the contemporary world to political action" (pp. 1–2). Fay saw the women's liberation movement as an exemplary model for his understanding of critical social science. He pointed to three dimensions of the women's movement that resonated with his commitment to praxis (i.e., a unified theory and practice): (1) the way social theory and social analysis contributed to the educative purposes of the movement; (2) the effect of consciousness-raising groups in transforming women's thinking and theorizing about themselves and society; and (3) how the women's movement addressed "the problem of resistance . . . of women who were initially opposed to it." Fay underscores how the women's movement was educative, transformative, and empowering—all characteristics of his view of critical social science. He maintains that "the experience of the women's movement is . . . a strong and positive one for those who wish to main-tain that broad-based social change can occur in an educative fashion. This movement is centered on the existence of critical theories which attempt to explain the existence of women in terms of false consciousness and social crisis" (Fay, 1987, pp. 112–114).

In the next section, we explore in more detail the "feminist challenge" (Nielsen, 1990, p. 5) to mainstream social science and its similarities and differences with critical and hermeneutical theory.

THE FEMINIST CHALLENGE TO MAINSTREAM RESEARCH

Following from the previous section, feminism can be situated as one of the postempirical, critical discourses. Like other critical theories in this cat-egory, feminist theory, for the most part, has objected to mainstream re-search that is influenced by positivist, instrumentalist epistemologies (Fay, 1987). Many scholars are convinced that "feminist research is contributing to a transformation of what traditionally has been called methods in the same way that feminist scholarship has transformed substantive academic disciplines and subdisciplines" (Nielsen, 1990, p. 1). Nielsen argues that feminism meets Kuhn's criteria of a genuine paradigm shift and claims that "the feminist challenge can be considered as more significant, more critical, and also more reconstructive than other critical traditions" (p. 18). Whether or not feminist research signals a true paradigm shift is arguable. Neverthe-less, one can point to very significant changes in the content and method of social science research that have resulted from feminist influences.

As noted, the interrogation of knowledge(s)—whose and how they are obtained—resonates with early developments in feminist social science. For example, the often-anthologized essay by Kathryn Pyne Addelson (1991), "The Man of Professional Wisdom," disrupts the received understandings of science and the "*unexamined* exercise of [male] cognitive authority" that accompanies it (p. 31). Addelson noted the lack of attention to "the so-cial arrangements through which scientific understanding is developed and through which cognitive authority of the specialist is exercised" (p. 17). Echoing the critique of androcentrism set forth earlier by feminist philoso-phers, most feminist researchers would agree "that the irreducible element in all feminist analysis is its focus on the distinctive experience of women—that is, seeing women rather than just men in center stage, as both subject matter of and creators of knowledge." This means that moving from the androcentrism of mainstream social science, both "what is studied . . . and how it is studied" are transformed. Not only are new subjects (such as rape, wife abuse, sexual harassment) considered significant enough to research, but also "reinterpretations, reconstructions, and reanalyses of existing data [can come] from the new perspective" (Nielsen, 1990, pp. 19–20).

Although gender analysis has become more legitimate as a category of inquiry and analysis for the social sciences, this was not always the case. Early researchers who argued against sexist bias and for incorporating women's perspectives often risked ridicule as bona fide scholars. Liz Stanley and Sue Wise (1990) note how some of the early feminist critiques of social science, including Jesse Bernard's 1973 essay, "My Four Revolutions: An Autobiographical History of the ASA," and their own 1979 work, "Feminist Research, Feminist Consciousness and Experiences of Sexism," "was a reaction against existing sexist bias within the social sciences, with the emphasis on exposing male-dominated disciplines and research behaviors" (Stanley & Wise, 1990, p. 21). Very early on, one dimension of this critique focused on the traditional view of objectivity and distance.

Dorothy Smith was one of the pioneers who "challenge[d] the epistemological basis of mainstream social science" as early as 1974. Working within the Marxist tradition, Smith offered a critique of "the norm of objectivity that assumes the subject and object of research can be separated from one another through a methodological screen" (Westkott, 1990, p. 60). Another challenge to objectivist methodology came with Jo Freeman's 1975 "study of the women's movement of the 1960s." Her groundbreaking research "was multimethodological and required the researcher's personal involvement—hardly the recipe for 'objective,' scientifically sound work" that is promoted as the ideal in traditional research (Nielsen, 1990, p. 6).

Ann Oakley's 1981 "study of the transition to motherhood" showed that the traditional "textbook advice about interviewing," which required a distancing between the interviewer and the subject to be interviewed, could adversely affect the quality of the interviews and the quality of the data to be gotten from the interviews. Oakley "got involved" with her interviewees, challenging "the subject-object separation" of standard research methodology (Nielsen, 1990, pp. 5–6). She was forced to get involved by the very relationships involved in her studies; the women interviewees demanded such a relationship. This work turned out to be innovative, pathbreaking not only in its conclusions but in its reflections upon method. The general epistemological critique posed by feminist philosophers, summarized previously in this book, therefore had real implications for research methods and modes of interpretation. Philosophical deconstructions of the subject-object dichotomy had direct consequences in terms of interview methods: the kinds of questions asked; the explicit inclusion of personal and emotional "data" as relevant to subjects that had previously been studied in a more distanced, impersonal manner; sharing research interpretations with interview subjects as a way of verifying them (and seeking to avoid a hierarchical researcher-subject power dynamic); and new forms of action research and other modes of inquiry that emphasize the collaborative relation between researcher and research subjects. For many (though not all) feminists, the adoption of such methods is an expression of their value commitments as well as their views of how to pursue inquiry most effectively: the two considerations are not separable.

Marcia Westkott's (1990) "Feminist Criticism of the Social Sciences," originally published in the *Harvard Educational Review* in 1979, was another early example of "feminist work to influence the social sciences." Westkott reminds us that "the critical dialogue that feminist scholars create within the various traditional disciplines . . . are not debates between outsiders and insiders. . . . The feminist debate arises because some of these insiders, who are women, are also outsiders." Traditionally educated women were beginning to see the limits of mainstream social science methods. Westkott goes on to discuss how "the debate becomes institutionalized within the academic sphere through women's studies programs and journals [and] begins to develop its own critical traditions" (pp. 58–59).

IS THERE A DISTINCTIVE FEMINIST METHODOLOGY?

We have focused primarily so far on the critique feminist researchers made of traditional social science. We now address the possible uniqueness of feminist inquiry as an alternative mode. Many feminist scholars have devoted considerable attention to the question of whether there is a distinctively feminist method of inquiry. In doing so, they have drawn on the important analytical work Sandra Harding (1987b) in distinguishing between "method, methodology, and epistemology" (see, e.g., Visweswaran, 1997; Gorelick, 1991; DeVault, 1996, 1999; Reinharz, 1992; Nielsen 1990). As Harding suggests, "issues about method, methodology, and epistemology have been intertwined with discussions of how best to correct the partial and distorted accounts" of traditional scientific research. As a philosopher, she argues that without clarity on these distinct concepts, it is "difficult to recognize what one must do to advance feminist inquiry" (Harding, 1987b, pp. 1–2). Hence, she sets out to delineate these terms and avoid conflating them (p. vii). In this section we review and rely on these categories to better understand the complexity of the feminist research process.

According to Harding, "a research *method* is a technique for (or way of proceeding in) gathering evidence." These "evidence-gathering techniques fall into one of the following three categories: listening to (or interrogating informants), observing behavior, or examining historical traces and records. In this sense, there are only three methods of social inquiry" (p. 2).

Harding goes on to distinguish method from methodology: "a methodology is a theory and analysis of how research does or should proceed." It is this concept, and not research methods themselves, that helps us grasp the true significance of feminist inquiry. What Harding and other "feminist researchers have argued [is] that traditional theories have been applied in ways that make it difficult to understand women's participation in social life, or to understand men's activities as gendered" (p. 3).

Finally, Harding maintains that "an epistemology is a theory of knowledge" that can answer "questions about who can be a 'knower' (can women?); what tests beliefs must pass in order to be legitimated as knowledge (only tests against men's experiences and observations?); what kinds of things can be known (can 'subjective truths' count as knowledge), and so forth" (p. 3).

As discussed in chapter 3, Harding reminds us that "feminists have argued that traditional epistemologies, whether intentionally or unintentionally, systematically exclude the possibility that women could be 'knowers' or *agents of knowledge*; they claim that the voice of science is masculine; that history is written from only the point of view of men (of the dominant class and race); that the subject of a traditional sociological sentence is always assumed to be a man." Feminist epistemology has offered us "alternative theories of knowledge that legitimate women as knowers" (p. 3).

Harding thinks that "there are important connections between epistemologies, methodologies, and research methods." However, she insists "it is *not* by looking at research methods that one will be able to identify distinctive features of the best of feminist research" (p. 3). Feminists, as we have stressed, can adopt a broad range of research methods in service of their larger purposes of seeking truth and transformation.

In the 1970s, in keeping with second-wave understandings of feminism, often "'feminist research' was defined as a focus *on* women, in research carried out *by* women who were feminist, *for* other women" (Stanley, 1990, p. 21). Clearly, this only captured part of the story, which was also about doing research in different ways. However, as Liz Stanley and others have indicated, there was an essentializing around categories related to women and gender that extended to particular research methodologies: quantitative methods were male and qualitative ones were female or feminist. Furthermore, it was assumed that feminist researchers were necessarily engaged in their work for explicitly political purposes—to effect social change, particularly for women. In retrospect, it is apparent that the research coming out of the early second wave of feminist history was undertheorized: it "relied on over-generalized and under-researched categories such as 'woman,' 'gender,' 'structure'" (p. 21). Both "feminism" and "research" were used in monolithic, totalizing ways; whereas even during this period the topics, methods, and perspectives of feminist research were not only multiple but were overtly given to experimentation with diversity and challenges to traditional categories and dichotomies.

With the advent of feminist materialist, postmodern, and poststructuralist theorizing, and the disruption of unitary concepts, feminist research was increasingly challenged to reflect the complex and contradictory characteristics of the material and social world in which women lived. The focus of feminist research shifted from women's experience to gender. As noted in our introduction, for many feminists, "to do feminist research [was] to put the social construction of gender at the center of one's inquiry" (Lather, 1991, p. 71).

According to Jayaratne and Stewart (1991), many feminists have concurred "that there can be no single, prescribed method or set of research methods consistent with feminist values" (p. 100). Virginia Olesen (2005), in her synthesis of feminist qualitative research for the third edition of Denzin and Lincoln's *Handbook of Qualitative Research*, echoes our earlier chapter when she reminds us that "feminism and feminist qualitative research remain highly diversified, enormously dynamic, and thoroughly challenging. Contending models of thought jostle, divergent methodological and analytical approaches compete, once-clear theoretical differences blur, and divisions deepen, even as rapprochement occurs" (Olesen, 2005, pp. 235–236). One area in which we see this diverse experimentation is in styles of research writing (which are not entirely separate from styles of inquiry):

critical autobiography, for example, valorizes "personal" writing and self-disclosure that would traditionally have been viewed as inappropriate to the distanced, impersonal tone of academic writing. Explicitly acknowledging aspects of one's identity and positionality relative to the topic under discussion is often viewed as a corrective to the "view from nowhere" and the false claim of objective authority. Personal narrative (for example, how and why one came to choose a particular research topic of question) is often regarded as unavoidably part of exploring the issue itself. As discussed previously in the context of standpoint epistemologies, the identity of the researcher is being made explicit and can itself become a criterion for evaluating the quality and reliability of the research results.

Olesen (2005) resists "positing a global, homogeneous, unified feminism." Yet, she sees that there are some common dimensions across "qualitative feminist research in its many variants, whether or not self-consciously defined as feminist." One commonality is that feminist research "problematizes women's diverse situations as well as the gendered institutions and material and historical structures" that frame them. Furthermore, "it refers the examination of that problematic to theoretical, policy, or action frameworks to realize social justice for women (and men) in specific contexts." And "it generates new ideas to produce knowledges about oppressive situations for women, for action or further research" (Olesen, 2005, p. 236).

Fonow and Cook (1991) agree that, even within these divergent paths, feminist theorists and researchers continue to seek broadly defining characteristics that distinguish "feminist attempts to transform the research process" (p. 1). For example, Cook and Fonow (1990) proposed "five basic epistemological principles" drawn from the work of "scholars who have analyzed feminist methodology" (p. 72). These principles include "acknowledging the pervasive influence of gender" (p. 73); "focus on consciousness-raising" (p. 74); "rejection of the subject/object separation" (p. 75); "examination of ethical concerns" (p. 77); and "emphasis on empowerment and transformation" (p. 79). Yet even here, we would suggest, examples can be found that belie one or another of these basic principles. Our own view is that this very tension, between trying to find unifying conceptions or themes, versus acknowledging difference, remains perhaps a deeper constitutive feature of feminist theory and inquiry—just as it has been a feature of the feminist political agenda more broadly.

This discussion of feminist inquiry is directed across the disciplines, not only educational scholarship (although several of the authors cited here specialize in education). This chapter constitutes a bridge, therefore, between the more philosophical issues discussed previously and the specific question of the impact of feminist theory and inquiry in the field of education. That is the primary topic of the concluding chapter.

REFERENCES

Addelson, K.P. (1991). The man of professional wisdom. In M.M. Fonow & J. Cook (Eds.), *Beyond methodology: Feminist scholarship as lived research* (pp. 16–34). Bloomington: Indiana University Press.

Bernstein, R. (1976). *The restructuring of social and political theory.* New York: Harcourt Brace Jovanovich.

Bernstein, R. (1983). *Beyond objectivism and relativism: Science, hermeneutics, and praxis.* Philadelphia: University of Pennsylvania Press.

Bloom, R. (1998). *Under the sign of hope: Feminist methodology and narrative interpretation.* Albany: State University of New York Press.

Britzman, D. (2000). "The question of belief": Writing poststructural ethnography. In E. St. Pierre & W. Pillow (Eds.), *Working the ruins: Feminist poststructural theory and methods in education* (pp. 27–40).

Britzman, D. (2003). *Practice makes practice: A critical study of learning to teach.* Albany: State University of New York Press.

Cook, J., & Fonow, M. (1990). Knowledge and women's interests: Issues of epistemology and methodology in feminist sociological research. In J. Nielsen (Ed.), *Feminist research methods: Exemplary readings in the social sciences* (pp. 69–93). Boulder, CO: Westview.

DeVault, M. (1996). Talking back to sociology: Distinctive contributions of feminist methodology. *Annual Review of Sociology, 22,* 29–50.

DeVault, M. (1999). *Liberating method: Feminism and social research.* Philadelphia: Temple University Press.

Fay, B. (1987). *Critical social science.* Ithaca, NY: Cornell University Press.

Fay, B. (1996). *Contemporary philosophy of social science.* Oxford, UK: Blackwell.

Feyerabend, P. (1975). *Against method.* London: New Left Books.

Fine, M. (1992). *Disruptive voices: The possibilities of feminist research.* Ann Arbor: University of Michigan Press.

Fonow, M. M., & Cook, J. (Eds.). (1991). *Beyond methodology: Feminist scholarship as lived research.* Bloomington: Indiana University Press.

Fonow, M.M., & Cook, J. (2005). Feminist methodology: New applications in the academy and public policy. *Signs, 30*(4), 2211–2236.

Freeman, J. (1975). *The politics of women's liberation.* New York: David McKay.

Gadamer, H.G. (1975). *Truth and method.* New York: Seabury Press.

Gorelick, S. (1991). Contradictions of feminist methodology. *Gender and Society*, 5(4), 459–477.

Habermas, J. (1971). *Knowledge and human interests*. Boston: Beacon Press.

Harding, S. (Ed.) (1987a). *Feminism and methodology*. Bloomington: Indiana University Press.

Harding, S. (1987b). Introduction: Is there a feminist method. In S. Harding (Ed.), *Feminism and methodology* (pp. 1–14). Bloomington: Indiana University Press.

Harding, S. (2004). *The feminist standpoint theory reader: Intellectual and political controversies*. New York: Routledge.

Jayaratne, T., & Stewart, A. (1991). Quantitative and qualitative methods in the social sciences: Current feminist issues and practical strategies. In M.M. Fonow & J. Cook (Eds.), *Beyond methodology: Feminist scholarship as lived research* (pp. 85–106). Bloomington: Indiana University Press.

Kuhn, T. (1962). *The structure of scientific revolutions*. Chicago: University of Chicago Press.

Lather, P. (1991). *Getting smart: Feminist research and pedagogy with/in the postmodern*. New York: Routledge.

Lather, P. (2007). *Getting lost: Feminist efforts toward a double(d) science*. Albany: State University of New York Press.

Nielsen, J. (Ed.). (1990). *Feminist research methods: Exemplary readings in the social sciences*. Boulder, CO: Westview.

Oakley, A. (1981). Interviewing women: A contradiction in terms. In H. Roberts (Ed.), *Doing feminist research*. London: Routledge and Kegan Paul.

Olesen, V. (1994). Feminism and models of qualitative research. In N. Denzin & Y. Lincoln (Eds.), *Handbook of qualitative research* (pp. 158–174). Thousand Oaks, CA: Sage.

Olesen, V. (2000). Feminisms and qualitative research at and into the millennium. In N. Denzin & Y. Lincoln (Eds.), *Handbook of qualitative research* (2nd ed., pp. 215–255). Thousand Oaks, CA: Sage.

Olesen, V. (2005). Early millennial feminist qualitative research: Challenges and contours. In N. Denzin & Y. Lincoln (Eds.), *The Sage handbook of qualitative research* (3rd ed., pp. 235–278). Thousand Oaks, CA: Sage.

Reinharz, S. (1992). *Feminist methods in social research*. New York: Oxford University Press.

Roberts, H. (Ed.). (1981). *Doing feminist research*. London: Routledge and Kegan Paul.

Stanley, L. (Ed.). (1990). *Feminist praxis: Research, theory and epistemology in feminist sociology*. London: Routledge.

Stanley, L., & Wise, S. (1983). *Breaking out: Feminist consciousness and feminist research*. London: Routledge and Kegan Paul.

Stanley, L., & Wise, S. (1990). Method, methodology, and epistemology in feminist research processes. In L. Stanley (Ed.), *Feminist praxis: Research, theory and epistemology in feminist sociology* (pp. 20–60). London: Routledge.

Stanley, L., & Wise, S. (1993). *Breaking out again: Feminist ontology and epistemology* (new ed.). London: Routledge.

Symposium: The personal and the political: Second-wave feminism and educational research. (2008). *Discourse: Studies in the Cultural Politics of Education*, 29(4).

Visweswaran, K. (1997). Histories of feminist ethnography. *Annual Review of Anthropology*, 26, 591–621.

Westkott, M. (1990). Feminist criticism of the social sciences. In J. Nielsen (Ed.), *Feminist research methods: Exemplary readings in the social sciences* (pp. 58–68). Boulder, CO: Westview.

CHAPTER 5

Feminist Educational Research

FEMINISTS, ESPECIALLY SECOND-WAVE FEMINISTS IN THE UNITED STATES, England, Canada, Australia, and New Zealand, have long seen education as a particularly fertile site for interesting and important research (Acker, 1994, pp. 18–19). This reflects, of course, the wider feminist concern with provoking critical reflection and consciousness raising, overlaid with the field of education as an area of special concern to women both as teachers and as parents. For example, Gabby Weiner (1995), a prominent British educational researcher who has written extensively about the connections between feminism and education, reminds us "that *feminism* has three main dimensions: *political*—a movement to improve the conditions and life-chances for girls and women; *critical*—a sustained, intellectual critique of dominant (male) forms of knowing and doing; [and] *praxis-oriented*—concerned with the development of more ethical forms of professional and personal practice" (pp. 7–8). For Weiner, these general dimensions of feminism are present in the particular research that she and other education feminists do.

A good deal of the second-wave feminist research that Weiner and Acker, among others, documented fell within the field of sociology of education and under the now-dated categories of liberal, socialist, and radical feminism. Weiner (1995) elaborated on this tripartite categorization; citing an earlier work with her colleague Madeleine Arnot (Arnot & Weiner, 1987), Weiner named three categories of feminism that they felt "had made the most impact on education: . . . 'Equal Rights Education' (namely liberal feminism), 'Patriarchal Relations' (radical feminism) and 'Class, Race and Gender: Structures and Ideologies' (Marxist/socialist feminism)" (Weiner, 1995, p. 52). As Acker (1994) notes, those identified as liberal feminists focused their research on "three major themes: (1) equal opportunities; (2) socialization and sex-stereotyping; (3) and sex discrimination" (p. 45).

This attention to equality offered "evidence of female disadvantages and gender discrimination in order to enable girls' and women's issues to be placed on the educational agenda" (Weiner, 1995, p. 2). Feminist researchers coming out of the liberal frame often focused "on girls' 'failure' or underachievement in the schooling systems and education more generally in order to campaign for change." The kind of change they sought, according to Weiner, occurred within the system "and with minimal disruption" (p. 67). Acker (1994) suggests that "in Britain, the discourse of equal opportunity, however flawed, is virtually the only one acceptable to the general public" (p. 45). Weiner (1995) supports this observation when she maintains that "*liberal feminism* . . . has arguably been the most enduring and accepted of all the feminisms" (p. 54) because it operated within mainstream vocabularies and values, such as promoting equal access to education for women and men. This is also due to the tendency of liberal feminists to work within existing social and political systems. As feminists interested in connecting theory to practice, and enacting change, the "strategies for educational change emanating from liberal feminism . . . attempt to alter socialization practices, change attitudes, use legal processes" (Acker, 1994, pp. 46–47). An example of liberal feminist scholarship is the volume by Myra Sadker and David Sadker (1994), *Failing at Fairness: How Schools Cheat Girls*. This collection includes twenty years of research documenting gender bias in schools and classrooms and concluding that girls are treated in a fundamentally unfair way by their teachers and through the curriculum.

At the same time, many feminists found the liberal feminist approach wanting, and criticized it for being "bourgeois and highly individualistic." In contrast to this liberal perspective, other feminist educational researchers thought more "revolutionary changes in economic, political or cultural life" were required (Weiner, 1995, pp. 53–54). One such group was the socialist-feminists, who had as a long-term goal "to remove oppression (in part by abolishing capitalism) . . . [and to focus] on women's position within the economy and the family" (Acker, 1994, pp. 47–48). Education feminists with a socialist critique—with what Madeleine Arnot and others have called "a political economy perspective"—sought answers to the question, "how is education related to the reproduction of gender divisions within capitalism?" (Arnot & Weiner, 1987, as cited in Acker, 1994, p. 48). This "reproduction theory" perspective is highlighted in the work of Kathleen Weiler, particularly in her 1988 study, *Women Teaching for Change: Gender, Class and Power.* Weiler clearly differentiates her research from liberal feminist analyses of schools. She maintains that the liberal approach "has tended to ignore the depth of sexism in power relationships and the relationship of gender and class . . . omits any class analysis" (p. 28). Building on a host of other socialist-feminist research, and on the dynamics of class, race, and gender, Weiler's study of women teachers "focuses on . . . the interplay of forces of social reproduction on the one hand and cultural reproduction and resistance on the other" (p. 57). Weiler studies the efforts of teachers and administrators to bring their feminist beliefs into contact with their practice in schools. Her understanding of feminist methodology, within a broad action research orientation, provides a more complete, sophisticated grasp of the complex workings of the classroom.

We have cited many examples here of how one's social-political framework will affect one's research questions and projects. Certainly this relation is evident in comparing the commitments of Marxist and socialist feminist research with liberal feminist work. The former, for example, tends to look more systematically at "how gender and power relations are continually reproduced in schooling." But, as Weiner (1995) suggests, the Marxist-socialist feminist research agenda, as critically important as it was for academics, was not particularly "influential for practitioners in the classroom" (p. 68).

Radical feminist educators, just like socialist feminists, sought "a fundamental change in the social structure, one that will eliminate male dominance and patriarchal structures" (Acker, 1994, p. 50). Focusing on "reproduction," they were most interested in how "the domination of men over women" was reproduced and how that reproduction was related to educational structures and processes (p. 50). Radical feminists employed "the concept of 'patriarchy' . . . to analyse the principles underlying women's oppression" (Weiner, 1995, p. 54). Viewing this oppression as "universal," these radical feminists felt that "women are *the* oppressed class" (p. 55). Given this view, radical feminists were not seeking equality in the sense of "sameness" as liberal feminists were; they were seeking "the abolition of gender as an oppressive cultural reality" (O'Brien, 1983, as cited in Acker, 1994, p. 50). To do this, they focused their inquiries on two major problems:

"(1) the male monopolization of culture and knowledge; and (2) the sexual politics of everyday life in schools" (Acker, 1994, p. 50). An example of this kind of radical feminist study of schooling is Dale Spender's (1982) *Invisible Women: The Schooling Scandal,* which addresses the disproportionate attention paid to boys by their teachers, at the expense of girls. Consequently Spender makes a feminist case for the benefits of single-sex education for girls.

Of course, as noted earlier, this tripartite categorization of feminist scholarship has been expanded by other feminisms, as well as being disrupted by feminist materialist, postmodern, and poststructuralist theory. There is now, for example, a great deal of exciting educational research employing a feminist-Foucauldian frame that examines, among other things, the discursive production of femininity, masculinity, and power.

A particularly strong body of work came out of Australia and England in the 1990s, including research by Bronwyn Davies (1989) on early childhood constructions of gender; Valerie Walkerdine (1990) on the fictioning of femininity; Alison Jones (1993) on becoming a girl; Erica McWilliam (1994) on the feminist construction of teacher education; and Sue Middleton (1998) on disciplining sexuality through schooling. They were joined by many feminist scholars in the United States, including but not limited to Leslie Bloom (1998) and Petra Munro (1998), who explored nonunitary subjectivity through their life history methodology and research on women teachers and administrators; Janet Miller (2005), with her work on poststructural autoethnography and autobiography; and of course, the powerful influence of Patti Lather (1991, 2007). Lather's demanding scholarship has contested the many facets of educational research and has offered useful challenges to feminist scholarship in particular. Her work over the past two decades has exhorted a generation of researchers to interrogate the assumptions embedded in traditional research methods as well as those employed by postpositivist scholars. Lather's insights into analyzing and synthesizing the theory-practice nexus and her commitment to informed activism in a range of domains are unmatched.

In looking historically at the developments in feminist research generally, and feminist educational research in particular, we can see shifts "from the position of having to provide evidence of female disadvantages and gender discrimination . . . to articulating a value-system and practice of feminist education that allows for greater sexual equality at the same time as acknowledging the differences that separate women." This "greater focus

on 'difference' . . . help[s] us clarify the 'problem of girls and women'"
(Weiner, 1995, pp. 2–3). At the same time, in dealing with both sameness
and difference, feminist researchers must confront "the issue of *universality
and diversity*," which Sandra Acker (1994) lists as "one of the 'paradoxes of
feminism'" (p. 53). She quotes at length from Nancy Cott:

> Rooted in women's actual situation, being the same (in a species
> sense) as men; being different, with respect to reproductive biol-
> ogy and gender construction, from men. In another complication,
> all women may be said to be "the same," as distinct from all men
> with respect to reproductive biology, and yet "not the same," with
> respect to the variance of gender construction. Both theory and
> practice in feminism historically have had to deal with the fact
> that women are the same as and different from men, and the fact that
> women's gender identity is not separable from the other factors that
> make up our selves: race, religion, culture, class, age (Cott 1986:
> 49). (Acker, 1994, p. 53)

As Weiner (1995) indicates, "Feminists working in education have certainly moved forward in the last two decades from the position of having
to provide evidence of female disadvantages and gender discrimination in
order to enable girls' and women's issues to be placed on the educational
agenda to articulating a value-system and practice of feminist education
that allows for greater sexual equality at the same time as acknowledging the
differences that separate women." She goes on to say that "drawing on the
work of feminists in the United States, France and Australia in particular,
a greater focus on 'difference' and 'explanation' now seems timely, in order
to help us clarify the 'problem of girls and women' and how we may move
forward into the 1990s and beyond" (pp. 2–3).

In Britain, for example, black feminists, upset with the "endemic nature
of both racism and sexism" in schooling, focused on "the *actual* experience
of black girls and young women in British schooling" (Weiner, 1995, pp.
68–69). And, in North America, black feminist Annette Henry (1998),
influenced by the work of Alice Walker, "use[d] womanism to denote [her]
own engaged scholarship in a search for theoretical paradigms starting from
the political, social, and cultural practice of Black women in the struggle for
educational and societal transformation." Her aim was "to generate theory
and raise questions about how Black women teachers' consciousness and

understandings at the intersections of race, class, gender, and culture contribute to and shape their pedagogical practice" (p. 3). More recently, critical race feminism has developed a space of theory and practice in which racial and gender oppression are viewed in relation to each other. For example, Venus Evans-Winter and Jennifer Esposito (2010) make the case for a multidisciplinary, coalition approach to educational research to better understand, validate, and transform the educational experiences of black girls.

Although we agree with Weiner (1995) that "equality issues are still vitally important to the work of education" (p. 6) and acknowledge the important early research done on women, schooling, and gender, we also want to emphasize recent feminist work that develops a multifaceted understanding of different gendered subjectivities, particularly as they are produced in schools, and their constitution within wider and more multifaceted dynamics of power. We also want to stress the value of this kind of research for teachers and other educators who may have come up against the limits of more traditional modes of scholarship. In the remainder of this chapter we recount several distinctive forms of feminist educational research in greater depth, in order to give the reader a grasp of why particular scholars have come to find them to be important lines of investigation.

GENDER IDENTITIES, DIFFERENCES, AND SUBJECTIVITIES

By now it is clear that feminism must be understood in its plural forms; no longer will the fiction of a unitary notion of woman's experience endure critical scrutiny or reflect lived reality. The intersections of race, class, gender, region, religion, and other identity and subjectivity positions have disrupted our understandings as they inform them. The theoretical and political frameworks of feminist materialism and poststructuralism, as well as postcolonial and critical multicultural theory, have produced some of the most cutting-edge feminist educational research in the past two decades. Too often scholars identified within the field of education are relegated to second-class status vis-à-vis scholars in philosophy or social science more generally (see Stone, 1994). Yet the education feminists highlighted in this chapter are, in our view, as theoretically sophisticated as any of the many feminist scholars from other disciplines cited in earlier chapters. We explore a few of them, including the groundbreaking work of Leslie Roman (1993), who developed a feminist-materialist approach to ethnographic research; the reflexive transformations of Deborah Britzman, who embodies a range of research stances; the innovative inquiry of Wanda Pillow (2003, 2004), who employs Foucauldian-influenced feminist genealogy in her research on educational policy and practice; the black feminist research and praxis of Annette Henry (1993, 1998); and the queer theory and research of Suzanne deCastell (1993, 1997).

Leslie Roman's feminist-materialist approach provides an excellent illustration of how research subject matter, political commitment, and methodology intersect. In her classic essay, "Double Exposure" (Roman, 1993), she reviews some of the difficult choices she faced as a committed feminist researcher studying adolescent girls from the punk subculture. She recounts two broad methodological stances from an ethnographic standpoint: "going native" versus remaining a "fly on the wall." The former involves strong identification with the research subjects and immersion in their context and activities; the latter involves maintaining distance and avoiding as much as possible any "contamination" that results in influencing the circumstances being studied, or being influenced by them. The former can provide thicker descriptions and richer emic interpretive understandings; the latter can provide more dispassionate analyses and a more etic distance from the ways in which research subjects might understand or evaluate their own activities.

Clearly, given the analysis in this book, this tension becomes especially problematic from a feminist point of view. As we have seen, denial of the subject-object duality and attempts at objectivity run deep in feminist views on epistemology and methodology. But a researcher in situ has to navigate the complex trade-offs between getting too close to her subjects while also maintaining sufficient trust and intimacy to develop a strongly intersubjective relationship with them (hence the title of Roman's essay). Roman recounts in rich detail her decisions about how to dress and how to interact with these young women, the emerging relations of trust she tried to build, and the mistakes she made along the way. Her essay is exemplary in recounting the real-world tensions, and difficulties, of navigating between going native and remaining a fly on the wall.

For feminists, moreover, there is the added consideration of personal and political affiliation and commitment. So when, for example, one of the young women she is studying tells her she is pregnant and wants an abortion, Roman faces a difficult choice about whether and how to get involved. The young woman cannot tell her family, cannot tell her boyfriend, and does not know who to turn to. A friend and mentor might already find this a difficult and conflicted choice; but a researcher is not normally expected to get involved in the lives of her research subjects in this way—and many would consider it a violation of research protocol to do so. What does Roman decide to do? Make a guess, then read the essay to find out.

Another feminist researcher committed to effecting change in the lived realities of teenage girls is Wanda Pillow. Pillow's (2003) work in feminist genealogy as methodology is an expansion of feminist Foucauldian research on the body, "read through and with race-feminisms" (p. 146). Having studied with Patti Lather, Pillow was influenced by Lather's methodological imagination as well as her grounding in Foucault's critical discourse analysis. This intellectual inheritance propelled Pillow, in her work on teen pregnancy policy in schools, "to shift the gaze of inquiry from the girls themselves to the discourses shaping and defining teen pregnancy, without losing the . . . girls' lived experiences" (p. 148). Not unlike her mentor and colleague, Pillow is both a research theoretician and a practical-empirical researcher. What is innovative and intriguing about Pillow's particular research is that she situates it squarely and unapologetically within policy studies—a generally conservative, male-dominated domain. In her 2004 book, *Unfit Subjects: Educational Policy and the Teen Mother*, Pillow "seeks to identify where the discourses of teen pregnancy are being formed, how they work, and what educational opportunities these discourses open up or delimit for teen mothers" (p. 8). In doing so, Pillow (2003) is able to move between "macro- and micro-level policy development" (p. 149) to address gaps in the received or "normal" narrative of teenage pregnancy (p. 148). Through her careful "discursive tracings," Pillow is able to demonstrate the lived consequences that result from how the teen mother and teen pregnancy are constructed. "Who we think the pregnant mothering teen is as a student, constructs the type of education she will receive" (Pillow, 2004, p. 111). Pillow was able to show the differential treatment girls received, depending on how they were seen by the school. If "teen mothers [were] described as and assumed to be 'poor students' . . . such discursive structures influence[d] a trend toward providing teen mothers with a basic, minimal education or with a vocational education" (p. 111). Pillow's (2003) research revealed that the typical narrative of the pregnant teen generally placed "responsibility on the teen mother herself without questioning the larger social constructions of teen pregnancy as a social, education and policy problem" (p. 148).

In her pathbreaking work, Pillow (2003) argues that "feminist genealogy cannot be separated from an understanding of the importance of the body in social organization, theorizing, power and practice" (p. 147). Consequently, the particularities of the teen mothers' bodies were important as well. In her work, Pillow insisted on threading critical discourse analysis with a powerful race critique in order to focus "specific attention upon the discursively structured raced, gendered and sexed body" (p. 146). This resulted in being able to analyze "how gender, race and sexuality impact the defining of the problem of teen pregnancy" (p. 152). One significant impact of Pillow's study has been to make "embodied analysis" an accepted methodology within policy studies research.

Annette Henry (1993, 1998), another feminist who connects political praxis with her research, brings a nuanced approach to her stance as an African-centered feminist standpoint researcher. She is acutely aware of the dangers of essentializing categories of race and gender, and says she is not promoting "universal, unified [identity] concepts" (Henry, 1998, p. 7). At the same time, Henry (1993) is committed to finding "new paradigms . . . new frameworks for understanding teaching and learning in multiracial urban contexts" (p. 207). Drawing on the "Afrocentric feminist epistemology" of Patricia Hill Collins, and embracing a sophisticated understanding of multiple identities, positionalities, and locations, Henry (1998, p. 215) sees the "possibilities in re/conceptualizing Black women's pedagogical practice" through her study of five black Canadian teachers.

As a feminist of color, Henry's (1993) research and praxis is an effort to "reconstruct Black realities amid social science categories based on European and patriarchal discourses" (p. 207). She does this through mainstream research practices including "participant observations of classroom practices, life-history interviews, teacher/student talk, student conversations, and conversations with the teachers and their practice" (Henry, 1998, p. 3). However, these typical research methods are put to use for advocacy purposes.

We noted in earlier chapters the intentional commitment of feminist researchers to correcting the lacks and distortions in mainstream social science; this commitment is manifest in Henry's work. Her engaged research requires her to ask her black women colleagues: "For whom is our work? For what purposes do we conduct our research? As political women of African descent, our research is necessarily a form of activism, revisionism, and reconstruction" (Henry, 1993, p. 218). And Henry's unabashed advocacy for black children and their families aims to rectify the effects of dominant exclusionary discourses and discriminatory policies and practices. Through what Henry calls "Black self-representation," she hopes to end the marginalization of African Canadian voices and experiences—a project that has real-world consequences for the life opportunities of black children—and work with the black community to "take back control" of their schools.

Cynthia Dillard is another critical feminist who places race and representation at the center of her work, particularly in the field of educational leadership. In her 2000 study of three African American women leaders, Dillard "use[s] the term *endarkened* feminist epistemology to articulate how reality is known when based in the historical roots of Black feminist thought" (p. 662). Relying on black feminist standpoint theory and epistemic privilege, Dillard uses interviews and the analysis of written texts to construct her narratives of her three subjects. Through her research process, Dillard acknowledged her relational responsibility to the women in her study, suggesting that "to know something is to have a living relationship with it, influencing and being influenced by it, responding to and being responsible for it" (p. 673). Citing Hill Collins, Dillard underscores the challenge they are both making to traditional notions of "value-free social science" (p. 674).

Deborah Britzman (1991, 1995, 1998, 2000, 2003, 2006), one of the most imaginative thinkers in educational theory today, is a feminist scholar who has transformed, and has been transformed, by a retheorizing of the research process. Her nonlinear scholarly trajectory moves from critical ethnographic study through (feminist) poststructuralist and queer accounts of educational practice and research, to psychoanalytic reflections on the "impossibility" of education.

Britzman's 1991 book, *Practice Makes Practice: A Critical Study of Learning to Teach*, and its subsequent 2003 revision, are instantiations of her commitment to rethinking and re-presenting her analysis, through a different frame. In the introduction to the 2003 revision, Britzman points out the limitations of dualistic thinking that saturated much of critical pedagogy and research, a framework that had shaped her own early scholarship. As we have traced in earlier chapters, poststructuralist theory was influencing a large segment of feminist and educational research by 2003, including Britzman's. In the retroactive deployment of poststructuralism to her earlier work, Britzman (2003, p. 5) was able to disrupt the neat dichotomies of progressive/regressive and success/failure to offer a more complicated, decentered understanding of her student teaching narratives. Her revision is a fascinating example of how the same data can be interpreted differently, depending on one's epistemological stance.

Britzman (2000) explores her theoretical shift in her reflexive essay, "'The Question of Belief': Writing Poststructural Ethnography." Drawing on Edward Said's critique of traditional ethnography, Britzman exposes the seductive power of the "straight version of Ethnography 101," showing how it relies on the "belief and expectation that the ethnographer is capable of producing truth from the experience of being there and that the reader is receptive to the truth of the text" (pp. 27–28). This "real" reading is disrupted by poststructural critique. With this different framework, Britzman offers an alternative view of her own research and has, subsequently, influenced others doing similar kinds of educational ethnography. Her interrogation invites us to "disrupt any desire for a seamless narrative, a cohesive identity, or a mimetic representation . . . [and reminds us that] 'being there' does not guarantee access to truth" (pp. 31–32).

In another play on the notion of "reading straight," Britzman (1995) asks, "Is there a queer pedagogy?" She was one of the earliest educational researchers to situate her work in the field of queer theory and to point out the "absence of gay and lesbian theorizing in education" (p. 151). For Britzman, it was not just the absence that was disturbing, but also that gay and lesbian experiences were "not given any thought. . . . [They were] unthinkable" (p. 151).

Britzman's (1998) explorations of the structures of intelligibility, the practices made possible by different discourses, and the effects of maintaining the unthinkable drew her to psychoanalysis as a way to understand "how education might be imagined" in our time (p. 3). Her disciplined imagination opened up "the question of education as a psychic event" (p. 3); in other words, "how does education live in people and how do people live in education?" (p. 5).

Perhaps playing off of Britzman's book title, *Practice Makes Practice*, another remarkable scholar, Suzanne deCastell, joined Britzman in being one of the first educational researchers to publicly study queer theory and pedagogy. In her 1993 article coauthored with Mary Bryson, "Queer Pedagogy: Praxis Makes Im/Perfect," deCastell "examines tensions between poststructuralist theories of subjectivity and the political/pragmatic necessity of essentialist constructions of identity" (p. 285). What is intriguing about this research is that it emerged from the lived reality of "being 'out' as 'queer' educators" (p. 286). DeCastell and Bryson reveal and reanalyze their own pedagogical practice in an attempt to transcend and transform (to no avail) essentialist understandings of identity and subjectivity. However, they declare that "in trying to make a difference we seem only able to entrench essentialist boundaries which continue both to define and to divide us" (p. 301). Consequently, they admonish those of us who "affirm dialogue[s across difference] and boundary-crossing" (p. 301). Their negative result resonates with the early work of Elizabeth Ellsworth (1989), who offered a scathing assessment of critical pedagogy when she asked, rhetorically, "Why doesn't this feel empowering?"

Extending this pioneering work in queer educational studies, Cris Mayo (2000, 2004, 2007, 2008) applies her philosophical training and critical research practices to the lived realities of lesbian, gay, bisexual, and transgender (LGBT) students in schools, and to the growing body of educational scholarship examining LGBT and queer issues. She deftly deploys Foucauldian discourse analysis through the nexus of power and knowledge, and his later work on the ethics of the self, to complicate and illuminate the formation of student sexual identities. In her study of gay-straight alliances, Mayo (2004) looks at "the central role of ethics in forming and maintaining communities" (p. 24). She argues that "because these groups are formed with the twin projects of challenging discrimination against sexual minorities and providing students with space to interrogate their identities and desires, the groups encourage students to see themselves as ethical actors and members of communities" (pp. 34–35).

Across this work, we see the intersection of feminist theory, feminist political practice, and research methodology and purpose. Avowedly committed, these feminist researchers are continually asking themselves how the doing of research is itself a manifestation of underlying assumptions about knowledge, dynamics of interrelation with those being studied, and a broader commitment to transforming social constructions of gender, class, race, and sexuality (and their manifold intersections). Their methods of investigation, and styles of writing, represent an ongoing experimentation with the standard genres of scholarship in the field—often taking the form of playfully or ironically turning dominant research conventions on their heads. Their work instantiates the broader principle of critical social research, that the purpose of inquiry is to intervene and transform, and not simply to understand, problematic situations within a distinctively feminist commitment to theory and practice. We hope that in this book we have provided a clear overview of the results of their work and its importance for educational research. In this, we have tried to write within a similarly reflexive and modest spirit, letting the theorists speak rather than imposing our own interpretations and categories on them.

REFERENCES

Acker, S. (1994). *Gendered education: Sociological reflections on women, teaching and feminism*. Buckingham, UK: Open University Press.

Arnot, M., & Weiner, G. (Eds.). (1987). *Gender and the politics of schooling*. London: Hutchinson.

Bloom, L. R. (1998). *Under the sign of hope: Feminist methodology and narrative interpretation*. Albany: State University of New York Press.

Britzman, D. (1991). *Practice makes practice: A critical study of learning to teach*. Albany: State University of New York Press.

Britzman, D. (1995). Is there a queer pedagogy? Or, stop reading straight. *Educational Theory*, 45(2), 151–165.

Britzman, D. (1998). *Lost subjects, contested objects: Toward a psychoanalytic inquiry of learning*. Albany: State University of New York Press.

Britzman, D. (2000). "The question of belief": Writing poststructural ethnography. In E. St. Pierre & W. Pillow (Eds.), *Working the ruins: Feminist poststructural theory and methods in education* (pp. 27–40). New York: Routledge.

Britzman, D. (2003). *Practice makes practice: A critical study of learning to teach* (rev. ed.). Albany: State University of New York Press.

Britzman, D. (2006). *Novel education: Psychoanalytic studies of learning and not learning*. New York: Peter Lang.

Davies, B. (1989). *Frogs and snails and feminist tales: Preschool children and gender*. Sydney: Allen and Unwin.

deCastell, S., & Bryson, M. (1993). Queer pedagogy: Praxis makes im/perfect. *Canadian Journal of Education*, 18(3), 285–305.

deCastell, S., & Bryson, M. (Eds.). (1997). *Radical interventions: Identity, politics, difference/s in educational praxis*. Albany: State University of New York Press.

Dillard, C. (2000). The substance of things hoped for, the evidence of things not seen: examining endarkened feminist epistemology in educational research and leadership. *International Journal of Qualitative Studies in Education*, 13(6), 661–681.

Ellsworth, E. (1989). Why doesn't this feel empowering? Working through the repressive myths of critical pedagogy. *Harvard Educational Review*, 59(3), 297–324.

Evans-Winter, V., & Esposito, J. (2010). Other people's daughters: Critical race feminism and black girls' education. *Educational Foundations*, (Winter/Spring), 11–24.

Henry, A. (1993). Missing: Black self-representations in Canadian educational research. *Canadian Journal of Education*, 18(3), 206–222.

Henry, A. (1998). *Taking back control: African Canadian women teachers' lives and practices*. Albany: State University of New York Press.

Jones, A. (1993). Becoming a "girl": Post-structuralist suggestions for educational research. *Gender and Education*, 5, 157–167.

Lather, P. (1991). *Getting smart: Feminist research and pedagogy with/in the postmodern*. New York: Routledge.

Lather, P. (2007). *Getting lost: Feminist efforts toward a double(d) science*. Albany: State University of New York Press.

Mayo, C. (2000). The uses of Foucault. *Educational Theory*, 50(1), 103–116.

Mayo, C. (2004). Queering school communities: Ethical curiosity and gay-straight alliances. *Journal of Gay and Lesbian Issues in Education*, 1(3), 23–36.

Mayo, C. (2007). Queering foundations: Queer and lesbian, gay, bisexual and transgender educational research. *Review of Research in Education*, 31, 78–94.

Mayo, C. (2008). Obscene associations: Gay-straight alliances, the Equal Access Act, and abstinence only policy. *Sexuality Research and Social Policy*, 5(2), 45–55.

McWilliam, E. (1994). *In broken images: Feminist tales for a different teacher education*. New York: Teachers College Press.

Middleton, S. (1998). *Disciplining sexuality: Foucault, life histories and education*. New York: Teachers College Press.

Miller, J. (2005). *Sounds of silence/breaking: Women, autobiography, curriculum*. New York: Peter Lang.

Munro, P. (1998). *Subject to fiction: Women teachers' life history narratives and the cultural politics of resistance*. Buckingham, UK: Open University Press.

Pillow, W. (2003). "Bodies are dangerous": Using feminist genealogy as policy studies methodology. *Journal of Educational Policy*, 18(2), 145–159.

Pillow, W. (2004). *Unfit subjects: Educational policy and the teen mother*. New York: Routledge/Falmer.

Roman, L. (1993). Double exposure: The politics of feminist materialist ethnography. *Educational Theory*, 43(3), 279–308.

Sadker, M., & Sadker, D. (1994). *Failing at fairness: How our schools cheat girls*. New York: Touchstone.

Spender, D. (1982). *Invisible women: The schooling scandal*. London: Writers and Readers.

Stone, L. (Ed.). (1994). *The education feminism reader*. New York: Routledge.

Walkerdine, V. (1990). *School girl fictions*. London: Verso.

Weiler, K. (1988). *Women teaching for change: Gender, class and power*. South Hadley, MA: Bergin and Garvey.

Weiner, G. (1995). *Feminisms in education: An introduction*. Buckingham, UK: Open University Press.

Weiner, G., & Arnot, M. (Eds.). (1987). *Gender under scrutiny:* London: Hutchinson.

Index

About the Authors

Wendy Kohli is professor of educational studies in the Graduate School of Education and Allied Professions at Fairfield University, Fairfield, Connecticut. Prior to that, Kohli directed the MST program in urban education at The New School for Social Research in New York City, taught in the Curriculum Theory doctoral program at Louisiana State University, and was first tenured and promoted at Binghamton University. Her scholarship has focused on critical theory, feminism, and critical pedagogy. She has published widely in a range of journals and books, including a volume she edited, *Critical Conversations in the Philosophy of Education.*

Nicholas C. Burbules is the Gutgsell Professor in the Department of Educational Policy, Organization and Leadership at the University of Illinois, Urbana-Champaign. His primary research focuses on philosophy of education, teaching though dialogue, and technology and education. He is the director of the Ubiquitous Learning Institute, dedicated to the study of new models of "anywhere, anytime" teaching and learning, given the proliferation of mobile technologies and pervasive wireless connectivity. He is also currently the education director of the National Center for Professional and Research Ethics, located at the University of Illinois. His most recent previous book (coauthored with Michael Peters and Paul Smeyers) is *Showing and Doing: Wittgenstein as a Pedagogical Philosopher.* He is the editor of *Educational Theory.*